# Southern Sun

# Southern Sun

## A PLANT SELECTION GUIDE

### JO KELLUM, ASLA

UP
M

UNIVERSITY PRESS OF MISSISSIPPI

*JACKSON*

*for Mr. Edward C. Martin Jr.*

*who claims the "C" stands for*

*crape myrtle*

www.upress.state.ms.us

The University Press of Mississippi is a member of
the Association of American University Presses.

Designed by Todd Lape

Manufactured in China by C&C Offset Printing Co., Ltd.

Page ii: Glossy abelia (*Abelia* x *grandiflora*)
Page v: Crepe myrtle (*Lagerstruemia indica*)

Photographs courtesy of Jo Kellum unless
otherwise noted

First printing 2008
∞
Library of Congress Cataloging-in-Publication Data

Kellum, Jo.
  Southern sun : a plant selection guide / Jo Kellum.
     p. cm.
  Includes index.
  ISBN-13: 978-1-934110-45-4 (cloth : alk. paper)
  ISBN-10: 1-934110-45-0 (cloth : alk. paper)
  ISBN-13: 978-1-934110-46-1 (pbk. : alk. paper)
  ISBN-10: 1-934110-46-9 (pbk. : alk. paper)  1.
Gardening—Southern States. 2.  Plant selection—
Southern States.  I. Title.
  SB453.2.S66K45 2008
  635.9′540975—dc22                    2007028021

British Library Cataloging-in-Publication Data available

XI      Acknowledgments

XII     Map of Southern Gardening Zones

XIII    Introduction

# Contents

# Bedding Plants

PERENNIALS: BEDDING PLANTS THAT COME BACK

| 3 | Autumn joy sedum | *Sedum spectabile* 'Autumn Joy' |
| 6 | Autumn sun coneflower | *Rudbeckia nitida* 'Autumn Sun' |
| 8 | Bee balm | *Monarda didyma* |
| 10 | Black-eyed Susan | *Rudbeckia fulgida* 'Goldsturm' |
| 13 | Bronze fennel | *Foeniculum vulgare* 'Purpureum' |
| 16 | Candytuft | *Iberis sempervirens* |
| 18 | Creeping phlox | *Phlox subulata* |
| 21 | Daisy | *Leucanthemum* x *superbum* 'Becky' |
| 23 | Garlic chives | *Allium tuberosum* |
| 26 | Mexican bush sage | *Salvia leucantha* |
| 29 | Purple coneflower | *Echinacea purpurea* |
| 32 | Queen Anne's lace | *Daucus carota* |
| 35 | Siberian iris | *Iris sibirica* |

ANNUALS: SINGLE-SEASON BEDDING PLANTS

| 39 | Elephant ear | *Colocasia esculenta* |
| 41 | Kimberly Queen fern | *Nephrolepis obliterata* |
| 44 | Lantana | *Lantana* hybrid |

# Shrubs

SHOWY SHRUBS

| | | |
|---|---|---|
| 49 | Anthony Waterer spirea | *Spiraea* x *bumalda* 'Anthony Waterer' |
| 52 | Bridalwreath spirea | *Spiraea* x *vanhouttei* |
| 54 | Burning bush | *Euonymus alatus* |
| 57 | Butterfly bush | *Buddleia davidii* |
| 59 | Doublefile viburnum | *Viburnum plicatum* var. *tomentosum* |
| 62 | Flower Carpet® rose | *Rosa* Flower Carpet® |
| 65 | Glossy abelia | *Abelia* x *grandiflora* |
| 67 | Korean spice viburnum | *Viburnum carlesii* |
| 69 | Winter jasmine | *Jasminum nudiflorum* |

EVERGREEN SHRUBS

| | | |
|---|---|---|
| 73 | Heller holly | *Ilex crenata* 'Helleri' |
| 76 | Nandina | *Nandina domestica* |
| 80 | Rosemary | *Rosmarinus officinalis* |

# Trees

SHOWY TREES

| | | |
|---|---|---|
| 87 | Crepe myrtle | *Lagerstroemia indica* |
| 91 | Ginkgo | *Ginkgo biloba* |
| 93 | Kousa dogwood | *Cornus kousa* |
| 95 | Kwanzan cherry | *Prunus serrulata* 'Kwanzan' |
| 98 | Lilac chaste-tree | *Vitex agnus-castus* |
| 100 | Saucer magnolia | *Magnolia* x *soulangiana* |

TREES FOR PRIVACY

| 105 | Leyland cypress | x *Cupressocyparis leylandii* |
| 107 | River birch | *Betula nigra* |
| 110 | White pine | *Pinus strobus* |

TREES FOR SHADE

| 113 | Drake elm | *Ulmus parvifolia* 'Drake' |
| 115 | Red maple | *Acer rubrum* |
| 117 | Sugar maple | *Acer saccharum* |

# Groundcovers

| 122 | Liriope | *Liriope muscari* |
| 125 | Sundrops primrose | *Oenothera perennis* |

# Vines

| 130 | Carolina yellow jessamine | *Gelsemium sempervirens* |
| 133 | Sweet autumn clematis | *Clematis flammula* |
| 136 | Trumpet honeysuckle | *Lonicera sempervirens* |

| 139 | Index | |

# Acknowledgments

Special thanks to my beloved Ray, for everything. To Emma, "Love y'all!"

Thank you to my mother, who read to me and understood when I agreed to pull weeds but ended up watching butterflies.

I am also grateful to many wonderful gardeners, both known and unknown to me personally. Among the many who shared their gardens with me, I thank Kay Hubbuch, Laura Jones, and Randy McManus.

To the Bruner family: May thoughts of John's sunny smile bring you the warmth of happy memories.

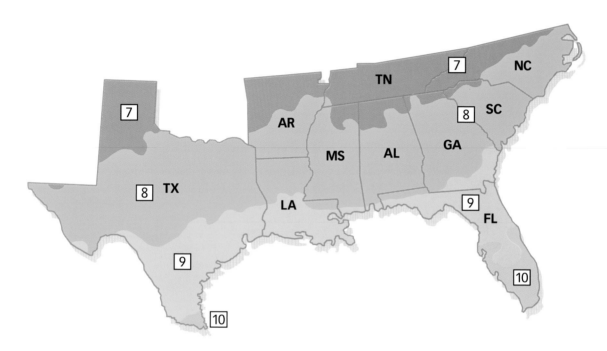

**MAP OF SOUTHERN GARDENING ZONES**

The upper portion of a zone is the area that is most
northerly. The lower portion is more southerly. This
can be confusing because lower zones have higher
zone numbers; nonetheless, within the following
pages, upper means northerly, in keeping with
horticultural tradition.

# Introduction

I always miss dessert. Any dinner party I attend sends me straight from the main course out to the garden, even if a flashlight is required. The questions of the evening alternate between "What should I plant there?" and "What's wrong with what I already planted there?" No matter how many gardening shows, books, and magazines there are, the basic need for assistance in figuring out what to plant where appears to be yet unfulfilled. The goal of this book is to offer advice on exactly that. If armed with enough information to put the right plant in the right place, landscaping satisfaction is well within anyone's reach. I wish I could attend your dinner party, and I'd love to see your garden—I'd even wander into the kitchen afterward to taste some of that dessert I missed.

The plants within these pages are arranged according to how they can be used in the landscape. Each plant description includes a range of zones in which it will grow. Look at the Southern Gardening Zone map to ascertain the zone in which you live. Any plant that includes your zone number within its range is suitable for your area. But individual landscapes and gardening zones are two different things, so read on to find out more about which conditions keep which plants happy. You'll find information about what different plants can do for you, too. After all, the goal is to put plants where you need them, where they belong, where they'll be easy to maintain, and where you'll enjoy them the most.

The whole idea behind *Southern Sun* is putting the right plant in the right place. Because sunshine in the South isn't like sunshine in other regions of the United States, this book strives to address gardening in sun as we know it. Particular attention is paid to issues of afternoon sun and morning sun, which have completely different effects on Southern landscapes and gardens. I do hope you'll find it helpful.

If shade is another challenge you face, take a look at *Southern Shade*, the companion book to this one. Though the hardest part about writing this pair of books was figuring out what to leave out, I've tried to include a range of plants large and small, colorful and not-so-colorful, in the hopes of answering questions and solving problems you may have in your own landscape. There are so many wonderful plants for the Southern climate. Perhaps you'll soon find a few new favorites.

# Bedding Plants

# Perennials

BEDDING PLANTS THAT COME BACK

# Autumn Joy Sedum

*Sedum spectabile* 'Autumn Joy'

Also sold as autumn stonecrop, showy stonecrop, *Sedum* 'Herbstfreude'

**GETTING ACQUAINTED**

Perennial bedding plant

2 feet high and wide

Succulent leaves are topped with blossoms on stalks; long-lived flowers progress from pale pink to rich rose and rust before turning brown

Moderate rate of growth

Tolerates drought, heat, cold, and salt

All-day sun, tolerates slight shade

Any well-drained soil

Good choice for slopes; rock gardens; perennial gardens; hot, dry beds; and containers that drain well

Pairs well with rosemary, garlic chives, evergreen candytuft, creeping phlox, Mexican bush sage, nandina, glossy abelia, black-eyed Susan, coneflower, ornamental grasses and cacti

Zones 3–9

utumn joy sedum is tailor-made for distracted gardeners like me. All you've got to do is put this plant in the right place and leave it alone. No need to water, fertilize, or fuss over it. This sun-loving perennial will come back year after year, blooming itself silly and thriving on neglect. That's my kind of plant.

Sedums are succulents, the camels of the plant kingdom. They store water for future use. Each spring, autumn joy sedum appears from last year's roots to produce a mound of thick, fleshy foliage and supple green stems. The leaves and stems are the hydration storage tanks for the plant. With its own built-in system for surviving drought, this perennial needs little water. In fact, it is essential to avoid supplying plants with too much water, as the roots of autumn joy sedum will rot in damp conditions. Soil must drain well to prevent moisture from lingering near roots. Dry soil that's naturally sandy or stony is best. Sunny slopes and raised beds where water naturally drains away are also good spots for succulents.

Sedums don't require much root room. They manage to flourish in pockets of soil on rocks, earning the nickname stonecrop. This ability means that sedums, including 'Autumn Joy', will thrive in containers placed in sun as long as roots don't become waterlogged. Choose pots or planters that have plenty of drainage holes. Fill containers with a light, dry soil mix. Perlite, an expanded volcanic rock that's extremely lightweight and looks like little white balls of destroyed Styrofoam, is useful for adding to potting soil for improving aeration around roots.

This plant thrives in poor soil that's sandy, rocky, or shallow. Water must drain away from roots for autumn joy sedum to thrive.

## CURING THE FLOPPIES

Always plant autumn joy sedum in as much sun as you can in order to avoid thin, spindly plants that reach for sunlight. However, even autumn joy sedums grown in adequate sun may become too tall and stagger under the weight of their blossoms. This usually occurs when plants are growing in rich, fertile soil—the kind that's ideal for most perennials but wrong for sedum. An autumn joy sedum that has been fertilized is particularly susceptible to becoming top heavy. You can stake such plants with tomato cages if you like. To prevent too-tall plants, refrain from feeding them. You can also move sedums to a sunny bed of dry soil that's lacking organic matter.

Or, you can pinch their heads off. Sounds cruel, but it works. When soft, new stems are about 8 inches tall, pinch them to within 2 inches of the ground. You can stop here or pinch again after stems grow a foot tall. Never remove more than 6 inches of growth. This technique forces sedums to produce numerous, shorter stems. Each stem grows its own flowers, so you'll get an extra abundance of blooms borne on sturdier stalks.

## FREE PLANTS

As an added bonus, it is a simple matter to turn autumn joy sedum clippings into new plants. Find a dry, sunny spot. Gently insert the cut end of a stem into loose soil to 1 inch deep. Anchor the stem in place with a rock. Water right away, then water sparingly. A new autumn joy sedum will take root from the cutting. You can do this with stems that have been pinched, clipped, or even broken from healthy plants.

## COLOR TIP

If your autumn joy sedum blossoms fail to progress to a hue that's richer and darker than the original pale pink, the plant is probably getting too much water. Dry conditions produce the best flower colors. Watering is unnecessary unless your garden is in the grips of a true drought. Sedums grown in semi-tropical climates may require some shelter from seasonal rains.

A

B

Whether in pots or beds, grow autumn joy sedum in the sunniest spot you can find. Hot afternoon sun is no problem for this tough plant. All-day sun is best, but sedum can tolerate a bit of shade as long as it is for less than half a day. When autumn joy sedum is grown in too much shade, plants become spindly, flowers are few, and stalks lean toward the light. Powdery mildew can become a problem on sedum grown in shady situations and roots are more likely to stay damp, causing plants to decline and die.

Fortunately, it is easy to dig up and move an autumn joy sedum that's growing in the wrong location. Whether you're relocating a plant or adding a new one to your garden, dig the hole in a sunny spot and amend the soil with sand and gypsum to improve drainage. Though most plants will benefit from a good dollop of nutrient-rich organic matter, don't waste it on autumn joy sedum. This succulent actually performs better in poor soil than in rich—plants grown in fertile soil often become too tall and flop over under the weight of flowerheads. Also, don't set your sedum too deep. Make sure the point where the stems emerge from the soil is set level with—not below— the surface of the surrounding soil. Do give newly planted sedums a few drinks of water to get them going, but after that, let plants depend on rainfall. Don't fertilize autumn joy sedum. Don't mulch around plants unless you substitute loose stones for organic matter.

By early summer, autumn joy sedum has outgrown its low, mounded shape by sending up numerous fleshy shoots. These are soon topped with light green buds bundled closely together, with a resemblance to broccoli. Buds change from green to pale pink and slowly open to form miniature galaxies tightly packed with five-pointed stars. When all the tiny flowers are open, autumn joy sedum blossoms take on a fuzzy look that shows off nicely against the plant's thick, rounded leaves. This stage would be reason enough to include

C

D

E

F

G

H

autumn joy sedum in your garden, but there's more to come. Pale pink blooms deepen in hue as summer passes, first becoming rosy in color, then deep, reddish pink. Butterflies and bees are strongly attracted to the flowers in summer and especially in autumn, when autumn joy sedum earns its name with blossoms that peak at their richest hues.

As autumn wanes, so too do the sedum's flowers, but first they darken yet again, this time to a rusty color that's quite suitable for the season. Flowers eventually dry on stalks as brown seedheads. If you're the tidy type, cut dead stalks to remove them (never pull them up by hand as it is much too easy to uproot the plant). Or, leave dried stalks standing through winter. Not only will they mark sedum locations so you don't accidentally dig these perennials up while they're dormant, but the seedheads also look lovely with a topping of snow. Trim away leftover stalks in spring when new leaves emerge. Then, remember to forget about autumn joy sedum. Neglect these perennials, and you'll enjoy another effortless year of color metamorphosis.

(A) Grow autumn joy sedum in full sun to enjoy months of flowers year after year.
(B) Autumn joy sedum returns from the roots each spring to produce a rounded mass of thick leaves.
(C) Stalks rise to form greenish buds that soon open to pale pink flowers.
(D) Flowers deepen to a rosy pink as they age.
(E) By autumn, blossoms are a rich red that darkens to rust as flowers dry in place on their stalks.
(F) Autumn joy sedum, rosemary, and Mexican bush sage make an easy combination that keeps garden beds from looking worn out and tired at summer's end. These three sun lovers will stay fresh through the first light frosts.
(G) The blossoms of autumn joy sedums attract bees, which sometimes spend the night on the pillowy flowers.
(H) With its lush mound of foliage, autumn joy sedum makes an attractive choice for a container. Choose pots that drain well so roots won't rot.
*Designer Randy McManus, Chapel Hill, North Carolina*

*Rudbeckia nitida* 'Autumn Sun'

Also sold as herbstonne, *Rudbeckia laciniata* 'Autumn Sun', autumn sun shining coneflower, autumn sun rudbeckia, herbstonne rudbeckia, cutleaf coneflower, green-eyed coneflower

## GETTING ACQUAINTED

Perennial bedding plant

5 to 7 feet high by 2 feet wide

Big golden yellow flowers with green centers appear atop tall stalks in late summer and into autumn

Rapid rate of growth

Resistant to insects and disease

Tolerates moderately dry conditions

All-day sun to mostly sunny

Any well-drained soil

Good choice for empty corners, backgrounds of sunny perennial beds, cutting gardens, and growing behind picket fences or beside arbors, pole-mounted birdfeeders, near porches and low decks

Pairs well with Mexican bush sage, rosemary, nandina, garlic chives, autumn joy sedum, sweet autumn clematis, lantana, butterfly bush, ornamental grasses, and sunflowers

Zones 3–9

Each cone-shaped center darkens from green to gold as blossoms age on their stems.

# Autumn Sun Coneflower

**M**ost gardeners will probably have to agree to disagree about this plant's name. Seems every nursery has its own version of what to call this big yellow bloomer, and that can make shopping a bit challenging. Here's how to make sure you're getting the right plant: The tag must include the name *Rudbeckia*. It also must include at least one of these two names, 'Autumn Sun' or 'Herbstonne'. If you find a combination of these names on the plant tag, you're set. Ignore other confusing nomenclature that may be listed and head for the checkout line.

Your new purchase will need a sunny spot when you get home. All-day sun is best, and mostly sunny is second best. Afternoon sun is fine for this heat-loving perennial that I'll call autumn sun coneflower—out of the choices of names, this one is particularly apt. Plants thrive in direct sun and feature bright, sunny yellow blossoms. The flowers open in late summer and early autumn. Flower centers elongate to form cones as the blooms age.

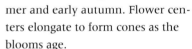

To add it to your garden, select a location where you need something tall to grow. Autumn sun coneflower starts off as a neat clump of big green leaves at ground level. Then stiff green stalks shoot up, some of them 7 feet tall. Fortunately, the stalks are branched and grow in clusters, making autumn sun coneflower less gawky than you might expect from such a skyscraper of a perennial. Each stem produces fresh foliage topped by a generous helping of flowers. The yellow petals surround pretty green centers in a haphazard fashion, with some petals held horizontally while others droop, as if someone hugged the blossoms a little too hard. Flowers aren't dainty—these beauties grow 3 to 4 inches across.

Both the tall stems and the big blossoms are surprisingly sturdy. An autumn sun coneflower in full bloom can come through a windy storm and hard rain nonplussed and none the worse for wear. Tall stalks rarely

**A**

**B**

**C**

**D**

**E**

require staking, either, if the plants are grown in full sun. The timing of the late-summer to early-autumn flowering—usually from about July through September and often into October—makes autumn sun coneflower a natural companion for Mexican bush sage. These two in bloom make a stunning purple-and-yellow combination. Both plants grow in full sun and well-drained soil, though autumn sun coneflower gets thirsty a little more quickly than its purple amigo.

Like other coneflowers, the yellow blossoms of this tall variety are long-lived. The green flower centers rise in maturity to form a cone that darkens to a golden hue. When the petals finally wither, you can cut autumn sun coneflower stems back to half their height in an attempt to trick your plant into putting on another flower show before frost. If you succeed, the second set of blooms is likely to appear on shorter stalks. Another option is to allow seedheads to dry on the stalks, attracting birds to your garden. (Hungry birds are always a good excuse for an untidy off-season garden.) Removing spent flowers and stalks right away is certainly permissible, as long as you clip the debris instead of pulling on it, as doing so may inflict root damage. Autumn sun coneflower is cold hardy. Foliage dies back in winter but the roots live on, generating new leaves each spring. In time, clumps widen to about 2 feet across.

**(A)** Flower centers start off green.

**(B)** Mature cones elongate and rise above the petals. If allowed to progress to brown, each cone will bear seeds.

**(C)** The large, dramatic yellow flowers of autumn sun coneflower attract butterflies initially, followed by birds that dine on the seeds.

**(D)** Though tall stalks bear some leaves, most of the foliage of autumn sun coneflower grows in a clump at ground level.

**(E)** Autumn sun coneflower grows up to 7 feet tall. Plants don't need staking but they may lean toward the light if their sun exposure is uneven. All-day sun is ideal, and there's no need to avoid hot afternoon rays.

## Bee Balm

*Monarda didyma*

Also sold as bergamot, Oswego tea

**GETTING ACQUAINTED**

Perennial bedding plant

3 to 4 feet high by 2 feet wide; forms spreading clumps

Shaggy rounded flowers, available in a range of colors, open on tall stalks in summer

Rapid rate of growth

Not drought tolerant

Mostly sunny; flowers best when partially shaded from afternoon sun

Any average garden soil that's kept moist

Good choice for butterfly and hummingbird gardens, cottage gardens, sunny perennial beds, herb gardens, or growing behind low picket fences

Pairs well with bronze fennel, Queen Anne's lace, black-eyed Susan, purple coneflower, butterfly bush, Siberian iris, nandina, and Flower Carpet® rose

Zones 4–9

'Kitty' is a pretty, purple-red cultivar of bee balm that is known for good mildew resistance.

Bee balm flowers attract, no surprise, bees. The sweetly scented, shaggy blossoms are also irresistible to hummingbirds and butterflies. Unfortunately, this plant sometimes attracts gardeners whose watering habits are, shall we say, theoretical at best. (I'm a card-carrying member of this category, myself.) Good-intentioned but busy homeowners who let their plants depend on rainfall alone can grow many plants, but bee balm isn't one of them. This tall perennial doesn't mind summer heat but it does require consistent moisture around roots. If you want plants that will bloom even when left untended in hot, dry soil, see the descriptions for Queen Anne's lace, autumn joy sedum, Mexican bush sage, and garlic chives.

But if you live where summer rains are a sure thing, or if you have naturally moist soil, a sprinkler system, or don't mind watering, bee balm is a great plant for you. Bee balm isn't a total diva—any average garden soil that's kept moist will do. Plenty of sun yields plenty of blooms, but a little shade from western rays in the afternoon helps to prevent soil dryness, thus keeping plants fresh and producing flowers. Removing spent blossoms keeps the flowers coming, too. You can deadhead consistently to enjoy a nonstop flower show for two months or more, starting in early to midsummer and lasting into autumn. Or, shear tops off of stalks all at once in late summer for a second flush of blooms.

Bee balm blossoms appear on the tops of branched stalks. Plants form tall clusters that are fully leafed from just below the flowers down to the ground. Bee balm is available in a range of flower colors, including white, pink, lavender, and red. The native species plant (*Monarda didyma*) only comes in red; keep that in mind if you're planting a wildflower gar-

A

B

den. All bee balms are kin to the mints, meaning these plants are both aromatic and apt to spread throughout beds. Fortunately, bee balm is easier to control than mint. Cut back clumps in autumn when plants become ratty; dig unwanted clumps to move or give away. About every third year, you'll need to dig up your largest bee balm clumps and divide them into smaller ones to keep the plants from wasting away from their centers. Divisions can be made in autumn or early spring.

**(A)** Bee balm mixes nicely with other tall sun-lovers, such as Queen Anne's lace. Hummingbirds love the blooms, which are also useful as cut flowers.

**(B)** Native bee balm (*Monarda didyma*) comes only in red, but hybrids extend the range of color choices. Members of the Oswego tribe are said to have taught colonists how to brew tea from the native plant following the Boston Tea Party.

## MILDEW TIPS

### PREVENTION

Humidity can promote the growth of powdery mildew on bee balm. Good air circulation is the best prevention for this fungal problem. Set plants in open spaces not hemmed in by solid walls, fences, or thick hedges. When dividing thick clumps of bee balm, replant the resulting smaller clumps 2 to 3 feet apart so air can flow among them. Avoid fertilizing plants too much, especially with nitrogen, which produces abundant lush growth that's susceptible to powdery mildew.

### TREATMENT

With hummingbirds, honeybees, bumblebees, and butterflies as fans of bee balm nectar, it is important to avoid chemical controls that can be hazardous to such creatures. A diluted milk spray is reputed among organic gardeners to be highly effective against powdery mildew. If your plants become distorted and coated with a gray powdery substance, you've got mildew. Cut all away all parts of affected plants and dispose of the debris off-site. (Don't compost it or leave it piled in a corner of your garden. Mildew spores can spread again and even overwinter.)

Next, mix up a batch of diluted milk. Powdery mildew is affected by an antimicrobial component of milk, lactoferrin, and other components of milk that produce oxygen radicals in natural light. Only one part of skim milk is needed to nine parts water to control powdery mildew on food crops. Many gardeners have adopted this formula for use on flowers. Diluted milk can be kept in your refrigerator for at least a week; a sour odor indicates the need for replacement.

Use a sprayer to apply the solution to the entire cut-down bee balm patch where powdery mildew was found. Morning is the best time to spray. For the most effective treatment, wait until rains have past and plants are dry. New shoots should emerge from the roots shortly. Reapply when new leaves appear. Repeat treatment weekly for two weeks. You'll enjoy healthy and chemical-free bee balm flowers, as will hummingbirds, bees, and butterflies.

## Black-eyed Susan

*Rudbeckia fulgida* 'Goldsturm'

May be sold as orange coneflower, gold-sturm, *Rudbeckia fulgida* var. *sullivantii,* or simply *Rudbeckia*

### GETTING ACQUAINTED

Perennial bedding plant

24 to 30 inches high by 18 to 24 inches wide

Golden, daisylike flowers with dark centers appear on stalks in late summer

Moderate growth rate

Tolerates heat, cold, and pollution

Insect and disease resistant

Plants reseed if seedheads are left to dry on stalks

All-day sun to partial shade; blooms best in sun

Average garden soil; not for wet soils

Good choice for entry areas, sunny beds, parking areas, roadside beds, cottage gardens, large containers, growing beside patios, porches, low decks, steps, and pool decks; include in cutting gardens and vegetable patches

Pairs well with Kimberly Queen fern, bronze fennel, rosemary, autumn joy sedum, purple coneflower, butterfly bush, garlic chives, liriope, Anthony Waterer spirea, bee balm, and ornamental grasses

Zones 4–9

The more sun black-eyed Susan plants get, the more flowers they produce.

Whether you're an experienced gardener or if you've never, ever grown a flower before, you'll be pleased with black-eyed Susan. This sun-loving perennial blooms profusely in hot weather. The flowers are borne on sturdy stalks and feature dark centers surrounded by a thick fringe of golden petals. Black-eyed Susans tolerate hot, humid summers and cold, harsh winters equally well.

The best way to grow black-eyed Susans is to raise a patch of them. Plants grown closely together choke out weeds and blend together to form a fluffy bed of green foliage. When cultivated in full sun, each plant will produce plenty of blooms; your bed will become a thick batch of bright golden flowers. This perennial blooms and blooms and blooms. Flowering begins in midsummer and continues right through the dog days of August into early autumn. If your plants take a break from blooming heavily, remove spent blossoms to encourage a fresh crop of flowers. Black-eyed Susan can tolerate shade for up to half a day, but flowering will be reduced.

You can buy black-eyed Susan plants in pots or you can purchase seeds. Either is fine, though the established root systems of potted plants means you've got a leg up in the gardening game. Just make sure your young transplants don't get too hot or too dry while they adapt to their new home in your garden. If you start with seeds, follow the directions on the seed packet. Keep seeds and the resulting sprouts moist (but not washed away with water) until rosettes of green leaves appear. After that, water plants during hot, dry spells when foliage and stems begin to droop. Skip watering if rain keeps plants from wilting.

After flowers fade in autumn, allow seedheads to dry on the stalks. Resist the urge to tidy up too soon. Instead, give plants a chance to drop

A

B

(A) Black-eyed Susan blooms heartily in late summer. Here, a backdrop of bronze fennel makes the golden flowers even more noticeable.
(B) This durable perennial will take whatever room it can get, so you can grow patches of black-eyed Susan in hot, narrow spaces.

## A TALE OF TWO SUSANS

Another great choice for the garden grows wild on the side of the road. Native black-eyed Susan (*Rudbeckia triloba*) has golden flowers like the cultivar R. *fulgida* 'Goldsturm', but you can tell the two Susans apart by their flower petals. The wildflower blossoms have short petals with rounded tips. The nursery-bred Susan has bigger flowers with long, pointy petals.

Native black-eyed Susan grows 2 to 5 feet tall. These wildflowers branch to produce plenty of flowers. Blossoms appear later in the season than they do on *Rudbeckia fulgida*. The wildflower blooms continuously for two to three months or longer. Native black-eyed Susan is heatproof like its cultivated cousin, but the wild plant is much more drought tolerant. It often blooms right through dry autumn days with little rainfall. *Rudbeckia triloba* may or may not come back from roots in spring; allow seedheads to dry on stalks so plants can reseed themselves for next year.

*Native black-eyed Susan (*Rudbeckia triloba*) is also sold as thin-leaved rudbeckia, brown-eyed Susan, thin-leaf coneflower, and branched coneflower.*

Fortunately, you don't have to choose between the two Susans. Including both the cultivated and the native plants in your garden will extend the blooming period, giving you a longer season of show. If you mix the plants, grow the tall wildflower behind cultivated black-eyed Susan. Grow both kinds in full sun in any well-drained soil. Native black-eyed Susan (*Rudbeckia triloba*) is becoming more common in the nursery trade. If you can't find it, check with a specialty nursery that sells native plants. You can also order seeds or collect them from the ripened seedheads by roadsides. Resulting plants may not bloom until their second year, but they're worth the wait. Self-seeding plants are likely to flower reliably each year thereafter if beds remain undisturbed.

seeds into the bed below. If stalks get too ratty to bear, cut the seedheads off and toss them into the bed and cover with a light coat of pine straw mulch. Snap or cut dead stems to remove them from plants. To avoid dislodging roots, don't pull up stalks by hand. Most foliage disappears in winter, but a good percentage of roots withstand cold winters. Sprouts from fallen seeds make up for the few plants that don't make it through severe cold. Seedlings help black-eyed Susan beds grow thick with plants, shading out weeds.

In spring, you'll need to gently remove any leaf debris that has accumulated in the beds so young plants can easily grow upward and reach sunlight. You won't need to do much more than that. Established patches of black-eyed Susan require watering only when wilting occurs; otherwise, you can count on carefree flowers.

A

B

C

D

(A) Black-eyed Susan grows with enthusiasm wherever its seeds land. Here, flowers took root between the sidewalk and a picket fence. The bright blooms mix nicely with the purple flowers of Brazilian verbena (*Verbena bonariensis*).
(B) Lawns and black-eyed Susans thrive in full sun, so you can easily grow a border of flowers beside grass.
(C) When left uncut, the dried seedheads of black-eyed Susan provide food for small perching birds, such as black-capped chickadees, purple finches, goldfinches, and wrens. Seeds also produce volunteer plants in spring.
(D) With sturdy stems and long-lived blooms, black-eyed Susans are ideal for cutting for arrangements indoors or out.

# Bronze Fennel

*Foeniculum vulgare* 'Purpureum'

Also sold as common bronze fennel, bronze sweet fennel, 'Purpurascens' Not to be confused with Florence fennel (*Foeniculum vulgare* var. *azoricum*) a vegetable grown for its edible bulb

P lanting bronze fennel in your garden is like cultivating mist. The feathery foliage is both fluffy and wispy. It makes a heavenly backdrop for large, coarse flowers such as black-eyed Susan or purple coneflower. Bronze fennel is so delicately soft you'll want to pat it. Grow it and you'll frequently find yourself identifying it for visitors enchanted by this perennial's fine, hazy foliage. Glossy, threadlike leaves start off as smoky purple or bronze plumes before fading to gray-green.

Bronze fennel is an herb, so you can use the leaves, stems, flowers, and seeds in all sorts of culinary delights. The flavor is often compared to anise, sometimes to licorice. But don't overlook this plant if you don't plan to use it in the kitchen—you'll love it in the garden as an ornamental addition. Bronze fennel is at home mixed into beds of perennials and annuals, so don't relegate it to the herb garden. In fact, fennel should be planted away from dill, with which it sometimes cross-pollinates unfavorably.

The size of bronze fennel varies in accordance with growing conditions. When grown in all-day sun in fertile soil, such as clay or well-prepared garden soil containing plenty of organic matter, bronze fennel may become 7 feet tall by summer's end. Regular watering promotes growth, too. Such size makes the feathery perennial ideal for filling empty corners, standing behind shorter perennials, or mixing with other tall plants. When grown in partial shade or in poor soil, bronze fennel may stay as low as 3 feet. Lack of water may stunt growth, too, though this plant doesn't demand constant moisture. Trimming lanky stalks promotes bushiness.

## GETTING ACQUAINTED

Perennial bedding plant

3 to 7 feet high by 1 to 3 feet wide

Feathery foliage is bronze when young, gray-green as plants grow taller

Moderate to rapid rate of growth

Tolerates heat and cold

May reseed aggressively in ideal conditions

Culinary uses

All-day sun to partial shade; larger sizes attained in all-day sun

Well-drained, fertile soil is best; any hot, dry soil will do

Good choice for perennial beds, cottage gardens, butterfly gardens, empty corners, backgrounds of sunny beds, and large containers

Pairs well with black-eyed Susan, purple coneflower, butterfly bush, autumn sun coneflower, bee balm, Queen Anne's lace, lantana, rosemary, and garlic chives

Zones 5–10

New growth is bronze but older foliage is green.

## BUTTERFLY FARMS

Bronze fennel is a larval host plant for eastern black swallowtail butterflies. The adult butterfly visits this perennial to lay its eggs. When caterpillars hatch, they're sitting right on a nutritious food source. Each tiny crawler starts off bumpy and black with a belt of white around its middle. Colors change to lime green with black spots or black striped with yellow dots. A steady diet of fennel foliage helps the caterpillars quickly grow large and plump. It is worth letting them decimate your plant to see them grow and know you're raising butterflies. Bronze fennel that has been chewed to bits by caterpillars always comes back the following year. Caterpillars ready to pupate usually crawl away nearly all at once to find suitable spots for cocoon building. To increase your garden's hospitality to butterflies, grow a nectar source, such as a butterfly bush, in close proximity to your bronze fennel.

A mature eastern black swallowtail, *Papilio polyxenes*, is attracted to the nectar of a butterfly bush. A nearby bronze fennel is a favored egg site for this butterfly species.

## CHILDREN'S PROJECT

Each generation of children delights in the transformation of caterpillar to butterfly. To witness the metamorphosis, wait until most of the caterpillars have disappeared from your bronze fennel. This indicates that they are ready to pupate. Stock a screened bughouse with a few fennel springs for the caterpillar's last-minute snacking and an assortment of sticks and leaves for housing. Cut a short stalk of fennel bearing a single remaining caterpillar and place it carefully in the insect house. Set the house in a shaded place where it won't be filled with water or be beaten by wind and rain. Your caterpillar will soon seal itself within a cocoon that looks something like a shiny seashell. Check on it daily, but have patience. When the new black swallowtail butterfly emerges, let your child open the door to free it right away. The butterfly may rest before trying its new wings, giving you a chance to admire it. Teach your child to refrain from touching it.

A

B

C

D

Bronze fennel blooms at the top of its stalks. Whether you leave the blossoms intact or cut them off is up to you. The lacy blooms are pale yellow and pretty and attract lacewings, a beneficial insect that eats the bad bugs. The flowers are edible, too, as are the seeds they produce. But seeds that fall from blossoms can yield a flock of unwanted seedlings. Plantlets are easy to remove from soft soil—in clay, not so easy. Seedlings are more prolific in sunny beds than in partially shaded areas. Some gardeners clip flowerheads early as a method of population control. Bronze fennel stops producing leaves when it blooms, so removal of buds to prevent flowering also encourages fresh plumes of foliage.

**(A)** Captured droplets make bronze fennel sparkle after a rain.

**(B)** Green and bronze-tinted feathery foliage occurs on the same plant. Clipped plumes of bronze fennel make slightly aromatic additions to floral arrangements.

**(C)** Lacy golden blooms open in mid-summer. The long-lasting flowers fade away in autumn, when they form seeds.

**(D)** The fluffy, misty-fine foliage of bronze fennel is attractive in any garden setting.

*Iberis sempervirens*

Also sold as evergreen candytuft

# Candytuft

**GETTING ACQUAINTED**

Evergreen bedding plant

6 to 12 inches high, spreads as much as 3 feet wide

Bright white flowers cover mounded plants in early spring

Drought tolerant

Resistant to insects

Moderate to rapid rate of growth

All-day to half-day's sun; needs early-spring sun to bloom

Any well-drained soil; not for damp or wet soil; grows fastest in soil that's rich in organic matter and drains well

Good choice for spilling over the tops of retaining walls, raised beds, or planters, growing on hillsides, in rock gardens, cottage gardens, tucking into crevices along walkways, filling in the front of planting beds; fine for restricted spaces

Pairs well with creeping phlox, autumn joy sedum, garlic chives, sundrops primrose, evening primrose, daisy, Siberian iris, bridal-wreath spirea, roses, and daffodils and other spring-blooming bulbs

Zones 4–8

Candytuft is tolerates heat and drought and resists insects, making it nearly carefree. It is a fine plant for draping over retaining walls, slopes, containers, and rocks. Here, it grows beside pink creeping phlox.

If you're seeking to add a bit of charm to your garden, candytuft is a plant that can do the trick. It has undeniable cottage-garden allure. Tucked here and there, growing in crevices in walls, tumbling over the tops of raised beds, or spilling onto walkways, candytuft contributes an enchanting finishing touch.

Anyone who thinks white is boring hasn't seen candytuft in full bloom. This little plant's snowy blossoms are blindingly bright and very showy.

Flowers cover the plant all at once in spring. The display doesn't last long, but the mounding foliage is attractive after blooming ceases. Candytuft is delightful on its own or paired with other spring bloomers, such as creeping phlox, daffodils, tulips, and hyacinth. Candytuft is also a good choice to grow with summer-flowering perennials that require the same growing conditions. Though such summery plants probably won't even emerge before candytuft blooms, that's the point. Candytuft will help you celebrate spring and disguise the absence of late-to-appear perennials. By the time the latecomers are in blossom, candytuft's flowers will be long gone, making the plant a good green, cushioned companion growing at the foot of taller plants that are showy in summer or autumn.

Luckily for beginners, this creeping perennial is easy to grow. Candytuft doesn't like wet soil, but other than that, it is not a picky plant. As long as you choose a well-drained spot that gets at least a half-day's sun, you're in business. All-day sun is ideal. Sunny sloping sites are perfect, as water runs downhill, leaving candytuft high and dry at the soil's surface. Candytuft's preference for good drainage is why this groundcover thrives at the tops of retaining walls, in raised beds, or tucked into rock gardens. It is a highly drought-tolerant little perennial. Though candytuft may appear weakened

A

B

C

D

after a hot, dry summer, chances are good that plants will bloom as well as ever the following spring.

Stems of candytuft grow outward from central roots, spilling sweetly over walls, stones, and the edges of planters. Avoid walking on plants. Pull any weeds that appear by first lifting candytuft's mat of foliage to reveal the weeds' roots. Each autumn, remove fallen leaves that may compress plants and deprive them of sunlight. Candytuft stays green year-round, though it doesn't have a dramatic presence in winter.

To keep growth vigorous, trim candytuft foliage ruthlessly after flowering finishes, every three to five years. (Use sharp hand pruners, not a string trimmer.) Leggy, thin plants indicate that more sun is required; move such plants to sunnier locations when temperatures cool in autumn. Transplanted candytuft will require more water than normal during the first few hot spells in its new home. You can also grow this plant in well-drained containers set in the sun. First the flowers and then fresh foliage will drape gracefully over the lips of pots.

(A) Zigzagging along the edges of walkways, spots of candytuft tucked here and there offer a quaint, cottage-garden look.

(B) Spring-blooming bulbs, like these tulips, pair well with candytuft.

(C) The dry conditions of sloping rock gardens are ideal for growing candytuft.

(D) When not in bloom, candytuft makes a mat of green foliage. Full sun and good drainage produce the densest greenery and most abundant flowers.

*Phlox subulata*

Also sold as thrift, moss phlox, moss pinks, ground pinks

**GETTING ACQUAINTED**

Perennial bedding plant

4 to 6 inches high by 24 to 36 inches wide; forms low, spreading mats

Early spring flowers create little carpets of color; available in screaming pink, lavender, white, red, and various combinations of striped petals or colored flower centers

Moderate rate of growth

Tolerates heat and cold

All-day to half-day's sun

Any well-drained soil; grows most rapidly in fertile soil with regular water

Good choice for slopes, rock gardens, cottage gardens, courtyards, containers, raised beds, planters, ditches, growing at tops of retaining walls, beside entries and walkways

Pairs well with candytuft, bridalwreath spirea, Siberian iris, saucer magnolia, pansy, Korean spice viburnum, rosemary, garlic chives, Mexican bush sage, and spring-flowering bulbs

Zones 4–9

If you can't make up your mind, plant a smattering of colors to blend and bloom together. White is the best choice for mixing with more vivid hues.

# Creeping Phlox

Spring has officially sprung when creeping phlox bursts into bloom. The five-petaled flowers are miniature and the plant is low—mere inches in height—but a creeping phlox in full bloom can knock your socks off. As the name suggests, this perennial creeps and crawls over whatever is handy: soil, stones, bricks, or edging. It cascades over retaining walls and spills out of planting beds to disguise the edges of walkways and patios. Tucked here and there, creeping phlox is an easy bearer of cottage-garden style.

The multitudes of flowers show their colors early in the season, marking a conspicuous end to winter's reign. The blossoms cover each low, matlike plant completely. The effect is a startling swath of color. But

because creeping phlox stays low, you'll need to plant it in a strategic location for maximum enjoyment. One old favorite gardening trick is to plant creeping phlox along the top of a retaining wall. There, water naturally drains away from roots, an agreeable situation for phlox. The plant creeps forward, launching itself over the top of the wall, and grows hanging down the wall's face. The look is stunning when creeping phlox is in bloom and charmingly casual when it is not. You can get a similar look by growing creeping phlox where it can ooze over the fronts of raised beds, planters, large containers, or sunny slopes. Plant it in an elevated position where it will grow downward. Or, set it close to the fronts of beds or beside edges of paving, where you're bound to see the blooms.

Creeping phlox may be considered an evergreen or semi-evergreen perennial. The quantity of foliage retaining its green color through winter is affected by the duration of freezes and the condition the plant was in before winter arrived. Beds of creeping phlox that have been dried out during summer will have less winter greenery than plants that produced lush growth due to regular watering. But even the most bone-dry creeping phlox

C

A

B

(A) Creeping phlox thrives in bright sun and dry soil, so it is great for planting on slopes and along the tops of retaining walls.

(B) There are few nontropical plants that can match the color intensity of plain old pink creeping phlox. This plant is also sold under the old-fashioned name thrift because you can buy a little and let it spread.

(C) For gardeners too squeamish for shocking pink, there are pretty pastel shades such as 'Emerald Blue'.

## PRUNING

Gardening wisdom calls for cutting creeping phlox back fairly hard after flowering ceases, removing anywhere from several inches of growth to a third of the plant. I can't bring myself to do it until my creeping phlox has turned gray and brittle from age or drought. Then I cut off the ugly stuff, marvel at the fresh green growth that follows, and chide myself for not being ruthless enough to trim it sooner.

## NAMED SELECTIONS

'BLUE HILLS': dark lavender-blue

'CANDY STRIPE': pink-and-white striped

'CORAL EYE': pinkish white with coral center

'EMERALD BLUE': pastel lavender-blue

'EMERALD PINK' AND 'FORT HILL': deep pink

'MAIDEN'S BLUSH': pink with red center

'RED WINGS': rosy red

'SCARLET FLAME': red-pink

'WHITE DELIGHT': white

CREEPING PHLOX

D

E

usually blooms heartily again in spring and sprouts fresh leaves. Plants are cold hardy and survive extreme winter temperatures.

The foliage is small and narrow, like something you'd find on an alpine plant. When the blooms are gone, creeping phlox makes a fine-textured mat of green in the landscape, attractive in a mossy sort of way. Fertile soil and even moisture produces flourishing greenery and the widest spreading growth, which in turn yields more flowers in springtime. But the main soil requirement of creeping phlox is good drainage—it can adapt to any soil that doesn't hold water. This plant will rot in wet soil or situations where water can't drain away from roots. Neglected and forgotten, creeping phlox grown along the banks of sunny ditches can remain for years after an old homestead has tumbled down, so you know it must be tough.

Full sun produces the best blooms. However, creeping phlox that relies solely on rainwater will benefit from a little dappled shade or shelter from hot afternoon sun. Dense shade makes plants sparse and flowering scarce—eventually, plants will fade away when grown in too much shade. Creeping phlox planted in the wrong place or that's becoming shaded by maturing trees can be dug and moved in autumn. (It is easy to remember when to transplant if you follow the rule of thumb that most perennials should be moved in the opposite season of bloom.) Gently lift the mat of foliage to locate the roots so you can move the entire plant. Lifting the foliage is also the best way to pull stray weeds by their roots without damaging creeping phlox.

(D) Bright white is another option. Here, creeping phlox dresses up a drainage swale.
(E) Creeping phlox forms a fine-textured mat of bright green foliage year-round, though it is not conspicuous in winter. Leaves are hidden by blossoms in spring.

# Daisy

*Leucanthemum* x *superbum*
'Becky'

Also sold as Becky Shasta daisy,
Shasta daisy 'Becky'

Love me, love me not: The cherished ox-eye daisy (*Leucanthemum vulgare*) found growing along roadsides in all fifty states is actually a British stowaway come to stay. Now common enough to be considered a naturalized citizen, the ox-eye daisy exhibits a remarkable ability to thrive untended, frequently earning it the mistaken distinction of wildflower. But ox-eye daisies are not natives, and they're listed as noxious weeds in some states, due to self-sowing flowers that crowd grazing grasses.

Shasta daisies offer hope for daisy lovers. This group of garden daisies manages to stay off most invasive plant lists. But Shastas have historically performed better in colder environments where plants are sufficiently chilled to produce blooms, making Southerner gardeners understandably less than enthusiastic about them.

Fortunately, along came 'Becky' and we've now got a Shasta daisy that's happy in hot, humid environments. Originally discovered in Atlanta, Georgia, the Becky Shasta daisy is now squarely in the love-me category of Southern plants.

The blossoms of Becky Shasta daisy feature the cheery bright white and sunny yellow color scheme that daisy traditionalists adore. The flower's main distinguishing characteristic is its size. Blossoms may reach 4 inches across and they're borne on sturdy stems about 40 inches tall. Becky Shasta daisies are durable and able to withstand pelting rain with no need for staking. The tall, stiff stalks make Becky daisies a fine choice for cutting. In fact, cutting the flowers makes this daisy produce more blooms, so clip plenty to enjoy indoors and to share. Blooms are long-lived in fresh arrangements.

Flowers start appearing in mid to late May and continue blooming throughout the summer. Deadheading will keep the flowers coming thick

## GETTING ACQUAINTED

Deciduous bedding plant (may remain green
   through mild winters)
Nearly 4 feet high and wide
Bright white flowers with sunny yellow centers
   open in summer
Rapid rate of growth
Tolerates heat, humidity, and cold
Resistant to insects and disease
All-day to half-day's sun
Any soil that's not wet
Good choice for sunny perennial beds, cutting
   gardens, cottage gardens, butterfly gardens,
   entries, and growing beside patios, pool
   decks, porches, or low decks
Pairs well with bronze fennel, Siberian iris,
   black-eyed Susan, purple coneflower, gar-
   lic chives, Mexican bush sage, and crepe
   myrtle
Zones 5–9

Daisies bloom profusely in full sun and attract
butterflies.

## WINTER DRAINAGE

Soil that holds moisture during cold weather can kill Shasta daisies. Both 'Becky' and 'Brightside' will grow in clay soil during the summer but they may not survive wet, cold roots. Tiny, tightly packed particles of dense soil can hold water underground. Such water becomes chilled in winter and can even freeze below the surface. If your soil is not naturally porous, consider growing Shasta daisies in raised beds, on slopes, or behind retaining walls, where water will easily drain away from roots. Planters and large containers filled with friable potting mix are another option. Amend naturally heavy soil with plenty of sand, gypsum, and large particles of organic matter, such as chunky compost or pine bark, before planting 'Becky' or 'Brightside'. Adding these components will increase air space within dense soil, permitting water to pass through.

## IDENTIFYING HEAVY SOIL

You can't improve a condition if you don't know you have it. Here's what experienced gardeners mean when they make reference to heavy soil. A shovelful of heavy soil really is heavier than a shovelful of light soil. Think about digging in sand as opposed to clay. Not only is sand easier to penetrate with the blade of the shovel, but it also makes a lighter load than clay does. That's because sand is composed of relatively large particles with a good bit of air between them. The finer, more tightly packed particles of clay have little air between them, making the soil stick together in a lump.

Most clay soils are rich in nutrients, and plenty of sandy soils are described as poor. One reason for the difference in nutrient levels is that water can run right through sand, leaching out minerals and washing away organic matter. Clay tends to hold water much longer, trapping it between the tiny particles. While this ability tends to preserve naturally occurring nutrients, it also causes poor drainage. Plants that prefer good drainage may decline or die when planted in heavy soil unless it is amended well prior to planting.

Most garden soil is somewhere in between the two extremes of sand and clay. If you squeeze a fistful of damp garden soil that's considered average, it will stick together a little in the middle but quickly crumble. If it makes a single ball, the soil is heavy and probably has poor drainage. If none of it sticks together, it's light, well drained, and isn't likely to be naturally fertile.

and fast—cut stems of spent flowers all the way to the ground. Conversely, allowing faded flowers to go to seed will discourage blossom production. In autumn, cut all stems to ground level after blooming ceases. Becky Shasta daisy is a sterile plant, so you can't grow plants from seed that are true to her characteristics. However, 'Brightside' is a descendant of 'Becky' that can be grown from seed. This cultivar is a little more compact, flowering on 32-inch high stems.

Becky Shasta daisies grow clumps of dark green foliage. Plants are long-lived when grown in well-drained soil. Dig up clumps about every three years to divide them. Discard dead material in the center of older clumps and separate young plantlets from the rootball to plant elsewhere.

(A) Becky Shasta daisy grows over 3 feet tall, putting blossoms at fence-top level for most picket fences.
(B) Clumps of foliage appears in early spring from the roots of Shasta daisies. Leaves may stay green through mild winters.
(C) The simple arrangement of white petals around yellow centers has long made daisies a favorite of many.
(D) Becky Shasta daisies make excellent cut flowers. Plants bloom more heavily when flowers are cut instead of left to go to seed on the stalks.

BEDDING PLANTS: PERENNIALS

# Garlic Chives

*Allium tuberosum*

Also sold as ornamental garlic, Chinese chives

If you've got dirt and sun, you can grow garlic chives. It's truly that easy. This plant is just happy to be here, don't mind me, and no water for me, thank you. It is the toughest of the tough. A close relative of culinary chives, garlic chives has edible leaves that can be used as seasoning but that's not why you'll grow it. The best feature of this sun-lover—besides the fact that it thrives on pure neglect—is its habit of blooming when other summer plants have given up hope of doing anything productive.

The flowers of garlic chives are borne in flat heads on stalks. They're brilliant white and showier than you might think. Each tiny blossom is star shaped and fresh and bright enough to add some much-needed twinkle to that pitiful in-between time in the garden when summer is supposed to be over but isn't and autumn is still an abstract concept. The plants themselves form less-than-impressive clumps of long, narrow leaves. They're green and plain, not even a rich shade of green. But boring also means inoffensive, so garlic chives can sit innocuously in your garden until it decides to curry your favor by flowering.

By the time August and September have rolled around, endless days of scorching heat and seasonal drought have separated gardeners into two categories: the devoted and the, shall we say, not-so-devoted. As a card-carrying member of the lazier category, I appreciate garlic chives' willingness to burst into bloom despite the fact that the hose is still coiled right where I left it last spring and other plants are as dried and withered as my good intentions. But plenty of more attentive gardeners love garlic chives, too. Plants grow in clumps, so blooms appear as snowy drifts that spread through beds.

## GETTING ACQUAINTED

Perennial bedding plant

12-inch high clumps of foliage double in height when flower stalks appear; width of clumps is determined by available space

Starry white flowers open in clusters on multiple stems in August and September

Moderate to rapid rate of growth

Very drought tolerant

Resistant to insects and disease

May reseed aggressively given ideal conditions

All-day to half-day's sun

Any soil except wet; grows fastest in soil that's rich in organic matter and drains well

Good choice for hot dry beds, sloping sites, containers, cottage gardens, cutting beds, patios, walkways, parking areas, and coastal landscapes; great for filling spots beyond the reach of a hose; fine for restricted spaces and urban conditions

Pairs well with rosemary, candytuft, creeping phlox, autumn joy sedum, autumn sun coneflower, black-eyed Susan, purple coneflower, Mexican bush sage, Queen Anne's lace, Anthony Waterer spirea, nandina, glossy abelia, butterfly bush, and culinary herbs

Zones 4–9

Garlic chives are a good companion for summer-flowering plants that are past peak by the time this perennial opens its white blossoms.

A

B

C

(A) Clumps of strappy foliage aren't much to look at through much of the growing season, but garlic chives send up stalks in the heat of late summer. The flowers freshen gardens at an awkward in-between time before cooler temperatures arrive.

(B) Garlic chives will grow anywhere it has soil and sun, even cracks in pavement or between stones.

(C) When you see green globes forming within flowerheads, it is nearly time to cut off blossoms if you don't want garlic chives to self-seed freely in your garden.

(D) Control the spread of garlic chives, if you wish, by removing stalks that look like this.

(E) The dried pods of garlic chives open to reveal black seeds. You can collect them to share or plant elsewhere. Or, let seeds sprout at will.

D

E

Its spreading ability may be garlic chives' only flaw. Some gardeners don't appreciate the young sprouts that grow from seeds dropped from flowers that have dried on their stalks. This is more of a problem for the devoted gardener than then not-so-devoted one. The former is more likely to have other plans for the space that new colonies of garlic chives inevitably occupy. Such a dutiful gardener is also more likely to have taken the trouble to prepare nice garden soil, unwittingly aiding this plant's spread by making it easier for seedlings to take root. All is not lost, however, if the devoted gardener will cut the flowerheads after petals wither to prevent plants from producing seed.

For the not-so-devoted gardener (you know who you are), the willingness of garlic chives to spread by seed is a bonus—free plants. The seeds of garlic chives are also more likely to encounter compacted soil in beds that are tended by lazier gardeners. Though this doesn't faze existing clumps of garlic chives, it does make it a little more challenging for seeds to sprout successfully, thus discouraging this plant's spread somewhat.

Garlic chives die down in winter and emerge again in spring. It is an optimistic plant that grows greenery earlier than many other perennials. Mild winters may leave clumps little changed, though foliage eventually withers to make room for fresh leaves. You can grow garlic chives in containers, on hot hillsides, mixed in with other sun-lovers, or squeezed into paving gaps in patios and walkways. It is a great plant for areas beyond the reach of the hose. Collect dried seeds in late autumn or early winter to start new patches elsewhere or to share with friends and neighbors. Scatter seeds in beds right away and scratch them lightly into the soil's surface.

The starry white flowers of garlic chives are good for cutting.

*Salvia leucantha*

Also sold as Mexican salvia, velvet sage

# Mexican Bush Sage

## GETTING ACQUAINTED

Perennial bedding plant

4 to 6 feet high and wide; largest sizes commonly attained in rare-frost and frost-free areas

Fuzzy purple flowers tipped with white top mounds of stalks in late summer and autumn

Rapid rate of growth

Resistant to insects and disease

Tolerates heat and drought

All-day sun to mostly sunny; the more sun, the better

Any well-drained soil; alkaline soil is fine, but not for damp or wet soil

Good choice for cottage gardens, backgrounds of sunny perennial beds, and foundation plantings in frost-free areas; attractive behind picket fences and beside arbors or pole-mounted birdfeeders

Pairs well with autumn sun coneflower, rosemary, nandina, garlic chives, autumn joy sedum, sweet autumn clematis, lantana, butterfly bush, and bronze fennel; good companion to distract attention from spent flowers of earlier bloomers such as black-eyed Susan, purple coneflower, and Anthony Waterer spirea

Zones 8–10; may come back in zone 7 if mulched well in autumn

Mexican bush sage is big, it's purple, and it blooms in autumn.

Mexican bush sage likes hot sun and dry soil. Hummingbirds and butterflies like Mexican bush sage. I like everything about this scenario.

This plant forms a large rounded clump of leafy stalks. The gray-green leaves have distinctive wrinkled surfaces. In late summer or early autumn when most gardens are looking a bit whupped, Mexican bush sage comes into bloom. Long, velvety purple spikes extend beyond the mound of foliage. Snow-white tips adhere to the purple; these are the true flowers, though the purple is what garners attention. Blooming continues unabated as long as the weather stays hot, which can be several months in the most southerly locations. Plants are sturdy enough to last through the first few frosts, but after that, they're done for the year.

Standing between 4 to 6 feet tall and wide, this fluffy perennial is large enough to perform shrubby duties in the landscape but it is not a year-round plant for most Southern gardeners. Only homeowners living in frost-free areas can count on Mexican bush sage to maintain a steady presence. Elsewhere, this plant is a perennial that dies down in early winter

and reappears in mid to late spring. In zone 7 (and even lower zone 6), Mexican bush sage is a tender perennial, meaning that with equal parts mulch and luck, gardeners in these colder areas can grow the same plants for several years until a drastic winter calls for replacements. Gardeners farther north grow it as an annual. According to new expert advice, Mexican bush sage should be left standing through the winter. Waiting to cut it to the ground in early spring instead of the previous autumn will prevent the hollow stems from becoming vessels for damaging ice. (Mulching roots well in autumn is still a good idea.) Immediately after spring pruning, feed plants lightly with a balanced fertilizer, such as 10–10–10.

It is optional, but a gentle all-over shearing in early summer is good for Mexican bush sage, regardless of whether the plant stayed green

A

B

C

(A) Although the white tips are the true flowers, purple spikes are the attraction of Mexican bush sage.

(B) Hot afternoon sun and dry soil agrees with Mexican bush sage; so does all-day sun. You can grow this perennial in semi-shade but the plant shape will become more leggy than rounded and flowering will be reduced.

(C) When cut, the blossoms of Mexican bush sage are long-lasting and stems are sturdy. Purple spikes retain their color in dried arrangements, too.

## NAMED SELECTIONS

'All Purple' (sometimes called 'Midnight') and 'Purple Velvet' both lack the white tips to flowers.

'Santa Barbara' is a dwarf cultivar that grows 3 to 4 feet high and wide, this selection may be more sensitive to cold than plants that mature at a larger size.

MEXICAN BUSH SAGE

Mexican bush sage attracts hummingbirds, bees, and butterflies wherever it is planted.

throughout the winter. This sage blooms on new wood, so trimming to encourage fresh growth will also create a good crop of color later in the season. Just take care to avoid cutting off any emerging blossoms. If you see fuzzy bundles clustered at the tips of stalks, you've waited too late, so skip pruning that year.

When adding Mexican bush sage to your garden, seek a spot that's sunny and dry. Make sure there's ample room for your Mexican bush sage to grow. Not only will it get tall, but it will also become wider the longer it's in the ground. Plants make nice round balls if they're not crowded. Starting new plants in spring will give them time to grow throughout the summer, and bigger plants mean more autumn flowers.

Newly planted (or newly moved) Mexican bush sages should be watered regularly for the first month or so, but allow roots to dry completely between waterings. After that, taper off watering so plants depend upon rainfall alone. However, there's nothing wrong with offering a plant a drink every now and then, especially during drought conditions. Just remember that overwatering Mexican bush sage can kill the plant, as roots will rot if they're consistently damp. Fortunately, this plant's desire for hot sun coincides nicely with a need for soil that's on the dry side. Avoid planting in heavy soil that doesn't drain well. If that's your garden's natural condition, grow Mexican bush sage in an extra-large pot, build a raised bed to improve drainage, or find a sunny slope where water will drain away from roots. Amend dense, clay soil with sand and chunky compost prior to planting. Alkaline soil is fine. In fact, Mexican bush sage thrives in soil that's a little on the limey side. If your plant is growing in highly acidic soil and the plant size or flower show is disappointing, apply a dash of lime to raise the soil pH.

# Purple Coneflower

*Echinacea purpurea*

Also sold as echinacea

P urple coneflower is a great perennial for beginners, rewarding minimal effort with prolific blossoms and butterflies to boot. It reseeds, so it's also a good choice for starting a garden on a budget. The easiest way to get growing is to plant a purple coneflower that already has leaves—purchase one in a pot or dig one up from a friend's garden. Tend one purple coneflower and it will produce enough seeds for patches of plants. Dropped seeds readily sprout—a good thing if you want more plants, but not so good if you don't. Fortunately, young plants are easy to dig up and relocate or give away.

Start purple coneflower in average to fertile garden soil. Drainage doesn't have to be ideal—purple coneflower will grow in clay—but soil that stays too damp can cause plants to decline and eventually die. Purple coneflower is unfazed by soil that's acidic, alkaline, or anywhere in between, so don't worry about your soil pH. Your new plant will need to be watered immediately upon planting and regularly for the first month or so of hot weather. An established coneflower can be sustained by rainfall alone until summer's peak. Then, water whenever the plant wilts to perk it up. In very hot weather, it's best to water purple coneflower in the morning to provide adequate moisture for the coming afternoon heat.

Purple coneflower can grow in all-day sun, though petal color fades somewhat. A little shade from direct sunshine in the afternoon keeps bloom colors bright. This agreeable perennial will also grow while receiving only a few hours of sun each day, though flowering will be reduced in shady conditions.

Foliage grows in thick, pretty clumps. By midsummer, sturdy branched stalks reach 3 feet in height and flowers form. Petals—actually known as ray flowers in horticultural terms—start off small and greenish. They grow

## GETTING ACQUAINTED

Perennial bedding plant

2 to 3 feet high and wide

Rosy purple flowers with orange centers bloom from midsummer into autumn

Rapid rate of growth

Moderately drought tolerant

Mostly sunny; flower colors are brightest when shaded from afternoon sun

Any soil that isn't wet

Good choice for entries, parking areas, sunny perennial beds, cutting gardens, wildflower gardens, butterfly gardens, meadows, and growing beside patios, porches, and low decks

Pairs well with black-eyed Susan, autumn sun coneflower, Kimberly Queen fern, garlic chives, Flower Carpet® roses, bee balm, Queen Anne's lace, nandina, crepe myrtle, lantana, rosemary, and Anthony Waterer spirea

Zones 3–9

Many species of butterflies feed on purple coneflower blossoms. This one is a great spangled fritillary (*Speyeria cybele*).

A

B

C

D

E

(A) Purple coneflower is an easy-to-grow perennial that thrives in sun and grows in just about every kind of soil.

(B) Bees are attracted to purple coneflowers, but they're generally too busy to bother humans.

(C) The petals of purple coneflowers start off green and upright, then turn colorful and point downward at maturity.

(D) The petals of purple coneflower are really a purplish pink. Flowers span from 1 to 4 inches across.

(E) Goldfinches and bluebirds feast on purple coneflower seeds when stalks are left uncut in autumn and winter.

bigger and brighter, ranging in hue from lavender to rich, rosy purple. As petals grow, they take a droopy position, surrounding the central disk like a stiff skirt. The rounded center becomes an elongated cone as the flower matures; this is where all those seeds are borne. The cone turns vivid orange, a bright contrast against the purple petals. This attractive display continues in earnest from mid to late summer into autumn. Bees and butterflies can't resist the blossoms. Flowers are long-lived on plants and even stay fresh for weeks indoors when cut stems are set in water.

When the long flower show has finally concluded, petals drop and seedheads remain on stalks. You can clip the bristly seedheads early to prevent plants from self-sowing and spreading. Or, wait until cones

F

G

are brown and dried to collect the seeds for planting or sharing. I leave the dead stalks standing. Goldfinches fill my garden in autumn, perching on the swaying seedheads, busily working away at the seeds within. Chickadees and bluebirds like the seeds, too. You can cut down the stalks after the birds have lost interest. But if the raggedy sight doesn't bother you, leave them standing until spring. That's what I did last winter, and the goldfinches swarmed through beds again during a warm spell, cleaning out leftovers they missed the previous autumn. Standing stalks also drop seeds, thickening existing patches with seedlings.

Plants die back in winter, followed by new leaves in spring. Purple coneflowers aren't picky about fertility, but a sprinkling of 10–10–10 granular fertilizer around each plant after leaves appear will encourage vigorous growth. Keep fertilizer off the leaves and water after the application.

**(F)** Black-eyed Susan and purple coneflowers are natural companions that bloom at the same time.
**(G)** 'White Swan' is a selection with creamy white flowers.

*Daucus carota*

Also sold as wild carrot

# Queen Anne's Lace

## GETTING ACQUAINTED

Biennial bedding plant (blooms during the second year; reseeds readily)

3 to 6 feet high by 1 to 2 feet wide

Large, elegant white flowers in summer; somewhat gawky plant form is softened by feathery foliage

Slow rate of growth the first year followed by rapid growth the next summer; takes two years to bloom

Very drought tolerant

Resistant to insect damage and disease

May be invasive

All-day sun is best; grows in semi-shade but flowering is reduced

Any soil except wet; poor, dry, and compacted soils are fine

Good choice for cottage gardens, sunny perennial beds, meadows, roadsides, natural areas, cutting gardens, and hot slopes; looks great with split-rail fences

Pairs well with bee balm, rosemary, Mexican bush sage, garlic chives, black-eyed Susan, autumn sun coneflower, purple coneflower, Flower Carpet® roses, and butterfly bush

Zones 3–10

The broad white flowers of Queen Anne's lace are landing pads for insects. Butterflies, bumblebees, and honeybees are attracted to the blooms. A pair beneficial bugs, antlions and green lacewings, come to feed on aphids. After ridding Queen Anne's lace of aphids, these useful insects will move to other nearby plants in search of additional prey.

The best place to obtain this plant is from the side of the highway. Queen Anne's lace grows wild in full sun in dry meadows and open right-of-ways. That's not to say it is a native plant. This lanky sun-lover is a European import that's made itself at home across the United States. It is sometimes listed as invasive, more problematic in some areas than others, and is pretty well entrenched in the weedy wildflower mix of the sunny South. It's doubtful that you'd do much additional harm by growing some in your garden, but care is needed to control its spread when seeds are set.

Queen Anne's lace is also known as wild carrot for its long taproot. In gardening terms, such a root means plants are difficult to dig up and transplant unless sprouts are quite young. But the seeds are easy to collect and easy to start, so that's the best way to go about growing your own patch of lacy summer flowers. The big white blooms adorn tall stalks in June and July, though at first flowers resemble little green bird nests. As the blooms mature, they unfold into flat or rounded white parasols, some as big as 4 inches across. The delicate blossoms signal that summer has truly arrived. Some Queen Anne's lace plants bear pinkish flowers. All plants produce numerous stalks, so one clump can yield more than enough blossoms for several good-sized bouquets. When flowers fade, they shed tiny knots of white, leaving an umbrella structure that's decorated with fuzzy seeds. The seedheads often curl up again, forming cupped brown nests by summer's end.

That's the time to go seed collecting. Dainty blossoms in your future and free seeds are ample incentive to pull over by the roadside with a paper bag in hand (watching for snakes all the while). As long as you don't disturb anything slithery, it is a worthwhile little field trip. Snap

A

B

C

D

E

entire seedheads off their stalks and into the bag. Just a handful of seed-heads will provide you with plenty of seeds to grow and share.

When selecting a spot for your Queen Anne's lace, look for an area in your garden that receives direct sun all day or close to it. This adaptable plant will grow in semi-shade, but blooming will be reduced and plants may lean toward sunlight. Look for a half-day's direct sunshine at a minimum and be assured that the hot sun of summer afternoons is fine. Poor, dry soil is just what this imported wildflower wants. Even compacted soil will do, although you should avoid wet or soggy areas.

Divide the seeds you've collected for your own garden into thirds. Sow a third of the seeds in your selected spot by scattering them on bare ground and scratching them lightly into the soil with a rake or garden fork. Next, sow another third of the seeds in the exact same area, but this time, simply scatter them. Don't scratch them into the ground. Save the

(A) The blossoms of Queen Anne's lace curl like nests before opening fully. Some curl up again when going to seed.

(B) The feathery foliage of Queen Anne's lace resembles carrot leaves and is a food source for caterpillars of eastern black swallowtail butterflies.

(C) The fuzzy stems of Queen Anne's lace are sturdy, but plants grown in indirect sun may lean toward the light and require staking to keep flowers from flopping in wind or rain.

(D) More gardeners are welcoming Queen Anne's lace in their landscapes than in years past, when the plant was strictly considered a weed.

(E) Collecting dried seeds from the wild is an easy way to add Queen Anne's lace to your garden. This plant is not to be confused with beggar's lice (*Torilis japonica*), which produces prickly seeds.

**CHILDREN'S PROJECT**

Cut blossoms of Queen Anne's lace soak up a lot of water through their sturdy stems. Children enjoy the transformation that occurs when generous doses of food coloring added to the water results in altered flower colors.

**CUT FLOWERS**

*Floral design by Emma Kellum*

Though the flowers of Queen Anne's lace are messy when they shed, they're lovely in short-term arrangements. The look can be summer casual, such as a jar of wildflowers, or more formal, as this pretty nosegay attests. It includes Queen Anne's lace, Apple Blossom Flower Carpet® roses, and English ivy.

**ROYAL ROOTS**

Once upon a time, lace-making was known as tatting. Only ladies with time on their hands could indulge in this handicraft of purely ornamental value. England's Queen Anne was apparently known for her tatting skills, and this lacey flower is named for her. Indeed, each delicate blossom resembles a fine, handmade doily. A dark cluster of purple-black petals in the center of each flower is said to be a reminder of a drop of blood that fell when the queen pricked her finger with a needle and stained a bit of lace she was making. Horticultural theory is less romantic, claiming these dark, sterile florets function to attract insects to the white flowers.

final third of seeds in a sealed container in the freezer until after the last frost next spring. Then, sprinkle the remaining seeds across the same patch of ground. Queen Anne's lace seeds grow without human assistance all the time, so it stands to reason that growing them in your garden shouldn't take much effort. In untended areas, this plant drops seeds in late summer to early autumn and grows new plants in spring, so leaving seeds exposed during winter is a logical attempt to mimic natural conditions. However, saving a portion of seeds to sow in spring is added insurance. Out of all of this, something is bound to sprout.

Queen Anne's lace is a member of the parsley family. The foliage is feathery and fine, light green, and graceful, which is a good thing, because that's all you have to enjoy during the first year Queen Anne comes to live in your garden. This plant is a biennial, growing for one full year before flowering and producing seeds. It is important to shake seeds from flowers down into beds to continue your ongoing patch (saving some for spring insurance planting) before you cut down stalks that have browned. Plants die after producing seed, so you've got to start the process over again. Fortunately, nature seems to work things out so you rarely have to spend a summer completely without flowers, though heavy blooming follows an alternate year pattern until you've got plenty of plants of different ages. Young plants may grow slowly during their first summer. They'll shoot up a thick, fuzzy main stem accompanied by plenty of lanky flower stalks the following year.

The trickiest thing about growing Queen Anne's lace in a garden setting is controlling where it appears. Don't be surprised to find this plant has migrated. You'll take care to plant it in one spot only to discover young plants in a different location next summer. Queen Anne's lace is a plant that spreads at will, so make sure you want it in your garden. Sprouts in the lawn can be mowed over (but may prove disturbing to lawn fanatics), and unwanted seedlings in beds can be pulled by hand or chopped with a hoe. I've dug up misplaced seedlings and moved them before the mower got to them, with mixed success.

It is permissible to treat watering Queen Anne's lace as a hit-or-miss operation, just as it is in open fields. Give your plants a drink from the hose while you're out watering something else, but let natural rainfall do the rest of the job. Don't overwater Queen Anne's lace, and don't fertilize it at all.

# Siberian Iris

*Iris sibirica*

Facial hair and flowers are not two topics normally considered together. But to examine the easy-to-grow Siberian iris is to first learn that it is a member of a clean-shaven clan, the beardless irises. The downward drooping part of the blossom, known as the fall, lacks the characteristic stripe of fuzz that gives bearded irises their claim to fame.

Furriness aside, many gardeners prefer beardless irises, particularly Siberians, for their low-maintenance beauty and range of flower colors. Siberian irises spread from horizontal roots known as rhizomes. You can start with a handful of rhizomes dug from a friend's garden, as I did, or purchase rhizomes or potted plants. Set rhizomes in a shallow pan of water to keep them happy while you dig planting holes or succumb to distraction and put off planting for a day or two. Soaking Siberian iris roots helps get them in the mood to grow in their new home. Plant rhizomes about 3 inches deep, and mix in some compost, rotted leaves, or peat moss if you feel so inclined.

Select a sunny spot within reach of a hose. Though fertile soil is ideal, Siberian irises adapt readily to average garden soil. Highly alkaline soil—the kind that has a pH level that makes it difficult to successfully grow azaleas without a huge struggle—is not recommended for Siberian iris, but that's about the only limitation. (Slightly alkaline soil is fine.) These tough little bloomers like soil that's wet but they'll live in dry soil with occasional watering, too. The fondness for damp soil means you can grow Siberian irises beside ponds and creeks and in boggy areas, though they're unlikely to thrive when grown directly in the water the way Japanese irises will. Siberian iris roots will rot in standing water.

## GETTING ACQUAINTED

Perennial bedding plant

3 to 4 feet high, forms spreading clumps

Richly colored flowers bloom in mid to late spring; attractive bladelike foliage stays green until the first frost

Early moderate rate of growth is followed by rapid increases in plant colonies

Resistant to disease and most insects; not as susceptible to borers as other irises

Tolerates heat and cold

All-day sun to partial shade; blooms best in sun but requires more water

Wide range of soils, from average to damp; slightly acidic soil is preferable

Good choice for entry areas, fronts of beds, pond sides, bogs, natural areas, groundcover beds, wet spots, and low-maintenance landscapes

Pairs well with saucer magnolia, Flower Carpet® rose, pansy, clematis, butterfly bush, and bronze fennel

Zones 3–9

The downward drooping petals, known as falls, of Siberian irises lack the fuzzy stripe found on bearded irises.

Purple and white Siberian irises are stunning
together. All-day sun and regular water produces
the most blooms in these easy-to-grow perennials.

All-day sun produces the largest bounty of blooms, but choose a blaz-ing hot spot only if it's naturally moist, covered by an automatic sprinkler system, or if you're willing to water. A site that's sunny for at least half a day will reduce the watering requirements and the quantity of flowers, so it is something of a trade-off. The best compromise is a mostly sunny area that offers some shade from hot afternoon sun in summer. You'll get plenty of flowers, and natural rainfall can take care of watering the plants. However, it would be rude to not offer Siberian iris a sip from the hose during extremely hot dry spells. This plant does give so much and asks for so little in return.

Siberian iris flowers are stunning, especially when beds are allowed to thicken naturally over the years, transforming from individual clumps into dense patches. The blooms appear in mid to late spring and are held high on sturdy green stems. Bright purple is the most common color and one that's quite satisfying. But hybridizers have had fun breeding Siberian irises for generations, so there's a wide range of hues from which to choose. White, yellow, lavender, pinkish purple, and dark rich purple are just a few of the standards. There's a slew of named selections that feature flowers that come in colors in between these hues.

The blooming period of Siberian iris is intense but brief, lasting for weeks, not months. But it is some consolation that the flat blades of foliage remain green all summer. The spiky appearance of the leaves is attractively coarse in texture, making Siberian iris a welcome addition to planting compositions long after the flowers have faded. Plants die down to the ground after the first frost. It is a good idea to cut away dead foliage and stalks and dispose of them off-site, as composting iris debris may create a culture for future problems. Roots survive through cold winters, so don't worry when the temperature drops.

Tips of green spikes emerge from beds in early spring. There will usually be more plants than the year before, so make sure you don't mind the spreading habit before introducing Siberian iris to your garden. You can let patches enlarge or invite friends to dig up unwanted strays for their own gardens. The first year of bloom will not be representative of the dense flowering in store for following years. Unlike their bearded cousins, Siberian irises rarely require dividing to maintain vigor. If you notice stems encircling a blank spot, lift and divide the rhizomes at any time except while plants are in bloom.

Siberian irises grown in partial shade flower at a reduced rate, but the blossoms are still pretty. The spiky foliage remains green all summer.

# Annuals

SINGLE-SEASON BEDDING PLANTS

# Elephant Ear

*Colocasia esculenta*

Everyone needs to grow elephant ears at least once. Hiding a fat brown tuber in the soil and being rewarded with huge floppy leaves on tall stems is too much fun for the money. Of course, you're not likely to stop with just one.

Elephant ears are tropical plants, and that's the look they contribute to the garden. But they aren't limited to theme gardens—the coarse texture of the leaves is showy in every setting. You can even include them in a formal garden for an eclectic, Victorian look. These large bedding plants look great beside water or even growing in pots set in ponds. The largest selections are useful for anchoring the backgrounds of flowerbeds. If watered regularly elephant ears will thrive in containers, so you can put them where you want to enjoy the large foliage.

To grow elephant ears, wait until nighttime temperatures drop no lower than 50°F. Then dig a hole that's 1 foot wide and deep and fill it with a combination of pine bark chunks, compost, peat, and native soil in equal proportions. This rich mixture will help nourish the tuber and retain moisture while the large hole and the air space between the particles will give water room to flow. The blunt, rooty end of the tuber goes down and the knobby side goes up, but if it all looks the same to you, simply lay the tuber horizontally in the half-filled hole. Include a scant teaspoon of slow-release fertilizer before covering the tuber with 6 to 8 inches of soil mixture. Soak the ground thoroughly but gently every few days. Continue watering when shoots appear. Soon, you'll have spear-shaped stalks that get taller by the day. The leaves arrive tightly wrapped but soon unfurl. Though elephant ears thrive in heat, they need plenty of water, so don't hold back. If the big leaves droop, get out the hose and they'll perk up quickly. A monthly feeding will help keep

## GETTING ACQUAINTED

Annual bedding plant; may come back in frost-free and rare-frost areas if mulched in autumn

2 to 6 feet high, depending on selection

Big leaves add a touch of the tropics; foliage available in shades of green and black

Rapid rate of growth

Tolerant of heat

Resistant to insects and disease

High water requirement

All-day sun to all-day shade

Well-drained soil, either poor or fertile

Good choice for providing a tall background for flowerbeds, filling empty corners, growing beside patios, decks, swimming pools; thrives at the edge of ponds or in pots set in the water; grow in containers or beds

Pairs well with Siberian iris, liriope, bronze fennel, Queen Anne's lace, bee balm, purple coneflower, black-eyed Susan, Kimberly Queen fern, lantana, and Anthony Waterer spirea; may provide shade for smaller plants that dislike direct sun

Zones 7–10

Elephant ears are favorite pond plants. Grow them at water's edge or in pots within the pond.

## OVERWINTERING TUBERS

Elephant ears are single-season plants in all but the mildest parts of the South. If you live where freezes are expected, you'll need to rescue the tuber or start over with a new one each year. Allow leaf stalks to remain attached to the tuber as long as possible before digging up the tuber for replanting the following spring. Resist the urge to remove declining foliage before the first frost. The leaves help feed the tuber, fattening it up for winter. After the first cold snap causes foliage to flop, cut stalks to ground level and carefully dig up the tuber. (Preparing the hole well at planting makes it easy to unearth the tuber in autumn.) If you slice it with the shovel blade, go ahead and cut the tuber apart. As long as there are eyes on the sections, they'll sprout. Trim remainders of leaf stalks as close to the tuber as you can without nicking it. Your tuber may have enlarged over the summer. If another smaller tuber is firmly attached, leave it alone. If a smaller tuber is loose, pull it off and you've now got two. It will take at least a day for tubers to dry thoroughly. Placing them on a slatted bench or clean, unused barbecue grill in the shade can improve airflow on all sides. For each tuber, fill a paper bag with dry peat moss or vermiculite and insert the tuber so it is cushioned on all sides and covered. Store closed bags in a cool (but not freezing cold), dry place—moisture and humidity can damage dormant tubers. Replant in the spring after the last frost. Plan to fertilize second-year tubers every three weeks throughout the growing season.

## NAMED SELECTIONS

'PAISLEY: also sold as imperial taro, eddoe, *Colocasia illustris*, or *Colocasia esculenta* var. *antiquorum illustris*; purple-black leaves are edged in bright green and striped with green veins; 1 to 3 feet high; tubers sold at some Asian specialty grocers; good for water gardens; may spread

'BLACK MAGIC': solid purple-black leaves and stems; 3 to 5 feet high

GIANT ELEPHANT EAR: also sold as *Colocasia giganteum*; solid green leaves are truly huge; 6 to 7 feet high

'RUFFLES': also sold as 'Ruffle Leaf'; green leaves have distinctive scalloped edges; 5 to 6 feet high

'JACK'S GIANT': green leaves; more than 7 feet high

'ROYAL CHO': blue-green leaves with purplish veins and black stems; 4 feet high

'MALANGA': also sold as *Xanthosoma atrovirens*, kimpol, Mickey Mouse cup, pocket taro, or dasheen; large, blue-green leaves; 4 to 5 feet high; tubers sold at some Asian specialty grocers

'VARIEGATED MALANGA': also sold as *Xanthosoma atrovirens* 'Variegatum Monstrosum' or 'Albomarginata'; striking foliage mottled cream and dark green; 4 to 5 feet high

elephant ears looking their best. To nurture the starchy tuber, use bonemeal or a water-soluble, high-phosphorus fertilizer—that's a product with a high middle number of the three. Follow directions and don't overdose your plant.

A

B

C

**(A)** Elephant ears are the living definition of coarse texture. Their big leaves add drama and contrast to any garden.
**(B)** Bright, hot sun is no problem for these tropical plants, but plan to water elephant ears a lot if they're not growing in a pond or damp spot.
**(C)** Looking for something different? Smaller selections of elephant ears will fit in a normal-sized pot.

# Kimberly Queen Fern

*Nephrolepis obliterata*

Also sold as Kimberly Queen sword fern, Australian sword fern, *Nephrolepis cordifolia*

Ferns arrive at nurseries by the truckload each spring to satiate our desire for leafy greenness. Boston ferns are the bright green ones that are usually sold as hanging baskets. They're very pretty but require shade and plenty of water. Now you can buy Kimberly Queen ferns, too. They're sold in pots, not baskets, and their fronds are deep, forest green. Unlike the Bostonians, her royal highness Kimberly can take the sun. This is endearing feature makes Kimberly Queen fern an extremely versatile plant for Southern landscapes.

Because any amount of sun or shade is agreeable to Kimberly Queen fern, you can grow it in those difficult spots that are sometimes shady and sometimes sunny. Sheltered areas such as porches and entry stoops are often thought of as shady, but slanting rays, particularly in late summer afternoons or evenings, can reach into such locations and scorch less-tolerant plants. Kimberly Queen takes it all in stride. You can even set one in full sun, though water needs will increase.

These ferns can do everything that Boston ferns can do except fill a hanging basket. Though Kimberly Queen's fronds eventually form a rounded globe of foliage, they start off growing more up than out. This, and their large size, makes these ferns impractical for hanging baskets. But such characteristics make Kimberly Queens good choices for growing directly in garden beds. Including a big fern in a bed of annuals or low groundcover is a quick way to dress up your landscape. These ferns aren't picky about soil, so you can grow them right in garden dirt. They'll require far less water than many annuals— impatiens, caladiums, and Boston ferns need to be watered much more frequently. Rainfall is usually adequate for Kimberly Queen ferns, though you'll need to supplement during hot dry spells. Whenever you've got the hose handy,

## GETTING ACQUAINTED

Annual bedding plant; may overwinter regularly in frost-free areas or occasionally in mild winters

30 to 36 inches high and wide

Dark green, stiffly arching fronds

Rapid rate of growth

Tolerates heat and sun

Resistant to insects and disease

All-day sun, mostly sunny, to partial shade

Average soil

Low water requirements

Good choice for growing in containers, planters, and beds; grow near entries, outdoor sitting areas, on porches, near swimming pools, and anywhere you need an accent

Pairs well with black-eyed Susan, purple coneflower, liriope, garlic chives, lantana, Flower Carpet® rose, evening primrose, sundrops primrose, nandina, crepe myrtle, rosemary, Anthony Waterer spirea, glossy abelia, and sun-loving annuals

Zones 7–10

Porches may be shaded for part of the day but heated by melting summer sun during the other. Kimberly Queen ferns are the perfect solution. These Australian natives are much more sun tolerant than their American cousin, the Boston fern.

A

(A) You can grow Kimberly Queen ferns in your garden, too. Plants won't survive winters in most of the South, so consider them as annuals that must be replaced each year. You'll get to enjoy green foliage until heavy frost.

(B) Because this fern takes sun, it is a natural companion to sun-loving flowering perennials such as black-eyed Susan and purple coneflower.

B

give them a good soaking. If the weather is such that sun-lovers like black-eyed Susans or purple coneflowers require water, then it is time to give Kimberly Queen ferns a drink, too. Ferns grown in all-day sun require more water than those set in partial shade.

These ferns hail from Australia, making them warm-weather visitors to your garden. Think of them as annuals—like pansies or petunias—and try not to feel too guilty when you send them curbside as winter descends. (Or, compost Kimberly Queen ferns for penance.) Overwintering them in frosty areas will require a warm indoor space with plenty of bright light and a high tolerance on your part for shedding fronds. Homeowners living where winters are mild can mulch ground-planted Kimberly Queens well in autumn and cross their fingers. Many gardeners find it easier to start anew each spring. You'll get your money's worth: Kimberly Queen contributes a nice ferny presence for months on end. Purchase them immediately after the last frost for maximum enjoyment. They'll last well into autumn or even early winter, tolerating light frosts before they finally succumb and turn brown and brittle.

Kimberly Queens are large ferns with stiff fronds that grow upward before arching over. The more space their roots have, the bigger your plant will grow. I've grown them in large pots 3 feet across. By the time winter arrived and I pulled them out, their roots had completely filled the pots and the fronds reached a good 3 feet beyond the container's lip.

The classic fern texture and the arching form of Kimberly Queen fern show up well when grown in urns, elevated pots, or other tall containers. You can also grow them in large, squatty pots or planters, too. I like to grow them in large pots and then set the pots in beds for an unexpected touch of formality at an entrance. Potted Kim Queens are also useful for filling empty corners on patios, raised decks, porches, and swimming pool decks. But there's no rule that requires this fern to be containerized—you can dig a hole and plant one directly in the ground, too.

*Lantana* hybrid

# Lantana

**GETTING ACQUAINTED**

Annual bedding plant; overwinters in frost-free
and rare-frost areas

2 to 3 feet high and wide, depending on selection

Bright little bouquets of flowers cover plants
during summer

Rapid rate of growth

Drought tolerant

Resistant to insects and disease

All-day sun to mostly sunny

Any dry soil, including poor, sandy soil; not for
wet soil

Plant only sterile cultivars, which are not
invasive

Good choice for parking areas, entries, sunny
perennial beds, butterfly gardens, roadsides,
slopes, and growing beside patios, swimming pools, mailboxes, porches, and low
decks; attractive in containers, hanging baskets, and planters; good for beach houses

Pairs well with black-eyed Susan, purple coneflower, Kimberly Queen fern, autumn sun
coneflower, garlic chives, Queen Anne's
lace, evening primrose, sundrops primrose, nandina, crepe myrtle, rosemary, and
Anthony Waterer spirea

Zones 7–10

You can mix lantana with other sun lovers.
Here, the yellow blossoms shine with violet
petunias. For quick effect, buy hanging baskets
of lantana. Remove plants from their containers
and plant in pots or beds.

L antana's motto seems to be "the hotter, the better." This plant thrives in bright sun and blooms steadily right through the heat of summer. Humidity, dry soil, reflected heat from paving, and car exhaust leave lantana unfazed. High or low soil pH are no problem, either. Most insects won't touch it. The only way you can go wrong with lantana is to plant it in the shade or in wet soil.

Add lantana to the sunniest spot you can find any time after last frost. This plant looks great growing in the fronts of beds, spilling over retaining walls or planters, and filling pots, window boxes, or hanging baskets. Grow it in hot, dry spots where other plants won't grow. Established lantana is very drought tolerant. Water young plants just until they produce new leaves, then let nature take over. Allow 4 feet between plants. If your

lantana outgrows its bounds or if flowering falters, cut plants back lightly. To make a go of overwintering lantana in zones 7 and 8, cut it back to the ground in autumn and cover with a mound of mulch or fallen leaves before freezing temperatures arrive. Uncover after the last frost and hope for the best.

Though the *Lantana* species plants that have escaped into the wilds of Florida are tall and woody and out of control, the newer named selections have been cultivated for compact growth. They're sterile, too, so the flowers won't produce berries. This means you won't have to go to the effort of cutting off berries to convince plants to flower again. Sterile lantana blooms nearly nonstop from the first heat wave until frost. Because the sterile plants don't set seed, they're not invasive, making them much more responsible choices than fertile-flower lantanas. Flower colors of sterile plants include gold, pink, lavender, and white.

As pretty as the prolific flowers are, they're not useful for cutting due to the strong, objectionable odor the plant bears. The smell isn't problematic outside, but if someone has brought lantana indoors you'll notice it when you walk in the door.

A

B

C

D

LANTANA

**(A)** Lantana can be as formal or as casual as you want it to be.

**(B)** Lantana doesn't wince at heat, bright sun, or car exhaust. You can grow it well beyond the reach of a hose, making this bright bloomer an ideal mailbox plant.

**(C)** Rounded bouquets of flowers have an unpleasant odor when cut and brought inside, so enjoy them growing in the fresh air.

**(D)** The *Lantana* species plant, sometimes called ham-and-eggs, is invasive in mild climates. Choose one of the newer, sterile selections of lantana instead.

## NAMED SELECTIONS

The following lantana cultivars are sterile, which means they are not invasive and they bloom continuously.

'NEW GOLD': golden flowers, up to 2 feet high

*Photo courtesy of Magnolia Gardens Nursery*

'WEEPING LAVENDER': lavender flowers, up to 2 feet high

'WEEPING WHITE': popcorn-white flowers, up to 2 feet high

'SAMANTHA': lemon yellow flowers, variegated foliage in two shades of green, 3 feet high

'DWARF PINKIE': pink-and-cream flowers, up to 2 feet high

## LEAFMINERS

The larvae of certain flying insects burrow inside lantana leaves, resulting in squiggly trails on foliage. The plant is rarely harmed to any great extent, but infestations are unsightly. To control leafminers, coat the undersides of leaves with horticultural oil spray or release parasitic wasps as a biological restraint. Severe leafminer infestations may require chemical control, such as the application of carbaryl (Sevin® dust) or permethrin (Ortho Bug-B-Gon Max Garden Insect Dust®).

Shrubs

# Showy Shrubs

# Anthony Waterer Spirea

*Spiraea* x *bumalda* 'Anthony Waterer'

Also sold as *Spiraea* x *japonica* 'Anthony Waterer', Anthony Waterer Japanese spirea

**Shrubs: Showy**

If you can get a grip on its unwieldy name, Anthony Waterer spirea is a great sun-loving shrub for your landscape shopping list. Delicate, willowy green foliage covers this broadly mounded shrub from spring until the first frost. Multitudes of pink flowers appear in flat clusters in early summer. Petal hue can vary among individual plants from medium pink to rose to deep magenta; all-day sun seems to produce the most richly hued flowers. This plant's welcome-to-summer blossom time makes it a particularly valuable addition to the landscape. When the spring blossoms of other plants are spent but many hot-season perennials are not yet ready to flower, Anthony Waterer spirea obligingly bursts into bloom. In autumn, leaf colors range from yellow to reddish purple. Plants are twiggy and bare in winter.

Grow Anthony Waterer spirea where it can get as much sun as possible. All-day sun is ideal. Foliage becomes sparse and flowering is thin on plants grown in shade. Partial shade for half the day is the maximum shade this shrub should receive. Anthony Waterer spirea likes it hot, so you can plant it in the full brunt of scalding afternoon sun.

Spireas aren't too particular about soil, and this one is no different. Any well-drained soil will do. Plants grown in rich soil with regular water will grow faster and bloom more heavily than those in poor, dry soil. However, Anthony Waterer is an adaptable sort and can make do in soil conditions that would make pickier plants shrivel. The only thing to avoid is a damp location. You'll need to supply young plants with regular water during their first hot season, but established plants are quite drought tolerant.

## GETTING ACQUAINTED

Deciduous shrub (bare in winter)

3 to 4 feet high by 4 to 6 feet wide

Profuse early-summer flowers range from pink to deep magenta; blossoms attract butterflies

Rapid rate of growth

Drought and heat tolerant

Resistant to insects and disease

Full sun to mostly sunny

Any well-drained soil

Good choice for growing between curbs and sidewalks, beside patios, steps, and walkways; shows off well in front of tall evergreen trees and shrubs

Pairs well with Flower Carpet® roses, butterfly bush, glossy abelia, nandina, black-eyed Susan, autumn joy sedum, creeping phlox, and candytuft

Zones 5–9

The profuse pink flowers of Anthony Waterer spirea have a delicately fuzzy appearance.

## KISSING COUSINS

Other Japanese hybrid spireas also thrive in full sun and well-drained soil. 'Goldflame' is known for bright gold to yellow-green leaves and rounded shape. In late spring, dark pink flowers and dark pink new growth contrast vibrantly with the golden green foliage. 'Goldflame' stays 3 to 4 feet high and wide, with little to no pruning required. It has pretty autumn color, and is bare in winter. Zones 4–9.

Limemound® is aptly named. The foliage is vivid chartreuse and plants form neat little mounds. This spirea grows 3 feet high, tops, and may be pruned in early spring to stay even lower. Flowers are not as showy as the foliage. Bare in winter. Zones 3–9.

A

B

c

Anthony Waterer spirea gets wider than it does tall, and this often surprises homeowners who have planted it too close to walkways. Each shrub can spread to a diameter of about 5 feet across, so set new plants 2.5 feet back from edges of walks, patios, driveways, and other shrubs. This spirea forms a pleasantly mounded shape that's 3 to 4 feet in height. As plants age, mounding becomes more dramatic, and a single plant can give the illusion of several grown together. Leaves and flowers cover these shrubs to the ground. This makes Anthony Waterer spirea a good foreground plant to grow in front of lanky roses or taller shrubs that have awkward bare stems at their bases, such as butterfly bush. It is also a good choice for growing beside steps.

Flowers appear on new growth. If you need to trim any wayward branches to control this shrub's size or shape, do so in early spring before leaves appear. Such timing will keep you from cutting off the current year's flower buds. Anthony Waterer spireas don't require a major pruning effort, as shrubs are naturally dense. Aged plants that have all but ceased blooming due to increased shade from maturing trees can be dug up in late winter and moved to a sunnier spot. Cut relocated shrubs back to within 8 inches of the ground to promote rejuvenated growth. Supply extra water throughout the first hot season in the plants' new location.

(A) Rusty brown buds turn deep pink before opening with lighter pink petals.
(B) The foliage of Anthony Waterer spirea turns yellow before plants go bare for the winter.
(C) Consider planting a summer-flowering shrub in a sunny spot instead of annuals. Anthony Waterer spirea bears pink blooms effortlessly year after year.

*Spiraea* x *vanhouttei*

Also sold as Vanhoutte spirea

# Bridalwreath Spirea

**GETTING ACQUAINTED**

Deciduous shrub (bare in winter)

6 to 10 feet high and wide

Showy white flowers cover arching branches
    in late spring

Moderate to slow rate of growth

Drought resistant

All-day sun to partial shade

Any soil that isn't wet

Good choice for slopes, large sunny beds,
    planting behind picket fences, low walls, and
    at the tops of retaining walls; plant one to
    stand alone as an accent; makes an attrac-
    tive informal hedge but won't block views in
    winter when leaves are down

Pairs well with spring-blooming bulbs, crepe
    myrtle, creeping phlox, candytuft, and
    Siberian iris; attractive before a background
    of Leyland cypress or white pine

Zones 3–8

Your grandmother called it bridalwreath. When this shrub is in bloom, it's easy to see why. Cascading branches tumble over one another, loaded down with little round white bouquets. You may find it for sale under another name: Vanhoutte spirea is the same plant. Whether you call it Vanhoutte or bridalwreath, this spring-blooming spirea is a durable plant that seems to be ever expanding in size. A large one in full bloom resembles a frothy fountain in the landscape. Flowering occurs in late spring, after leaves have appeared.

Fading flowers have their own beauty. After a grand show, the white petals drop, leaving fuzzy-looking circles of antiqued brown. The spent blooms are delicately pretty, like old lace. Eventually, the green to greenish blue foliage is all that's left for summer. Autumn color is a respectable yellow. Bridalwreath is naked all winter, but resist the urge to get out there and whack at it with the clippers. If you chop those bare stems, you'll be sorry come spring when your plant doesn't bloom and the graceful sprays have been replaced with awkward sprouts.

Bridalwreath spirea is a shrub that anyone with sun and space can grow. A spot that gets full sun is best because that's what yields the most flowers. However, partial shade is acceptable, though plants need at least half a day's sunshine to bloom. It doesn't matter whether available sun reaches bridalwreath spirea in the morning or the afternoon, so there's no need to shield it from hot, western rays. Established plants are tolerant of both heat and drought and actually prefer soil that's a little on the dry side. Bridalwreath thrives on neglect.

This shrub grows as a big, arching clump. The rate of growth is moderate, but that can fool you—when it seems that your shrub is grown, it

The fountain-like form of bridalwreath spirea is not for the faint-at-heart gardener. If you want a tidy, compact plant, don't buy this one.

continues to slowly increase in size. In time, a bridalwreath spirea can grow 10 feet high and perhaps wider. When adding bridalwreath to the landscape, allow a minimum of 6 feet of clearance for height and spread. It's a mistake to think you'll keep the size in check by pruning. Ruthless annual pruning will prevent flowering because buds form on old wood. Don't even try to shear this shrub into a formal shape. You'll end up with a bundle of sticks with little foliage. It is fine to selectively remove stray branches here and there (make cuts immediately after flowering), but bridalwreath is an unruly shrub that's best left alone. Plant it where you can celebrate its large size and vigorous sprays.

**(A)** The buds and blooms of bridalwreath spirea mingle on the same arching stalks as flowering gets underway in spring.
**(B)** The foliage of bridalwreath spirea is an unremarkable bluish green in summer. The serration of leaf edges is an identifying characteristic.
**(C)** Rounded clusters of blossoms resemble tiny bridal bouquets.

## WHEN IT REALLY IS TOO BIG

If prune you must, cut old, gray stems back to within 1 foot of the ground in late spring. This will promote fresh growth, though bridalwreath spireas going through this sort of rehab remain awkward in appearance for quite a while and won't bloom until they regain some size. Don't do this more than once or twice during the shrub's lifetime. If the plant is truly too big for its space, you might want to consider moving it instead of fighting the size battle for years. Bridalwreath spirea is a tough plant, so moving it is certainly worth a try.

To relocate a bridalwreath spirea, dig it up and move it immediately after severe spring pruning. The roots of an old plant will make quite a large ball, so make sure you don't cut too close to stems with the shovel blade. You'll probably have to wiggle the rootball onto a tarp and drag it its new location. Set the shrub in a new hole at roughly the same level as it was growing before. Don't plant it too deeply, and don't leave the rootball sticking out of

the ground. Water frequently after transplanting to encourage new root growth. A bridalwreath that has been moved is likely to survive just fine, but remember to keep it watered in hot, dry spells during the first summer in its new home.

## HOUSEKEEPING

Fallen oak leaves often get caught in the thick cluster of bridalwreath spirea's stems. Accumulated leaf debris may eventually prevent sunlight from reaching the center of the shrub. It doesn't take long to clean fallen leaves out by hand, if you do so when they're dry and easy to dislodge.

*Euonymus alatus*

Also sold as winged euonymus, winged burning bush

# Burning Bush

**GETTING ACQUAINTED**

Deciduous shrub (bare in winter)

10 to 15 feet high and wide; named selections grow more slowly and can be maintained at smaller sizes through pruning

Leaves turn brilliant fiery red in autumn

Slow rate of growth

Tolerates urban conditions

All-day sun to partial shade; more sun yields brighter autumn color

Any well-drained soil

Good choice for hedges, background plantings, parking areas, growing beside fences; don't grow burning bush near woodlands in cool regions as plants can spread, becoming invasive and crowding native species

Pairs well with lawns, nandina, ginkgo, and sugar maple; Leyland cypress grown behind burning bush makes an excellent seasonal contrast of dark green and bright red

Zones 4–8

Fire engine red autumn foliage is the claim to fame of burning bush. As soon as temperatures drop at night, the solid green leaves of this shrub begin to turn. Sunlight aids the process, so plants grown in full sun turn the brightest red. The leaves of burning bushes grown in partial shade will change colors, too, but the transformation may occur unevenly. Leaves facing the sun will turn red before leaves in the shade do, so the color seems to creep over plants in partial shade, although it's still an attractive process. Shrubs grown in dense shade turn pinkish or an undesirable faded yellow—it is best to avoid planting burning bush where it receives less than a half-day's direct sun. Burning bush

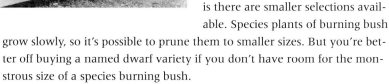

can take the heat, so there's no need to position it away from western afternoon sun.

Burning bush cultivars are bred to grow more slowly and stay smaller than the species, *Euonymus alatus*. This is good to keep in mind while plant shopping. Unless there's an extra name on the plant tag indicating that the shrub is a cultivar, expect burning bush to get very big—close to 15 feet high and equally wide. The good news is there are smaller selections available. Species plants of burning bush grow slowly, so it's possible to prune them to smaller sizes. But you're better off buying a named dwarf variety if you don't have room for the monstrous size of a species burning bush.

All types of burning bush thrive in any soil that's not wet. Dry soil is fine, though shrubs require supplemental water during droughts. The almost-dainty foliage of burning bush is arranged attractively in horizontal layers, though the shrub itself is quite round. When bare in winter, the V-shaped trunks and stiff branches are noticeable in the landscape, especially when lined with snow. Older branches are trimmed with corky ridges called wings, another feature that's evident in winter. Dwarf cultivars have fewer wings than the species plants do. With their large size, burning bush species plants are often grown as hedges and buffers. This is a good

Burning bush gets large, so give it room to grow. Dwarf selections grow more slowly and lend themselves better to pruning for size.

A

B

C

D

**(A AND B)** Cool autumn temperatures and sunlight turn burning bush from its summertime green to bright red. The more sun burning bush receives, the redder it turns in autumn.

**(C)** Corky ridges called wings grow along mature stems of burning bush and are especially noticeable in winter.

**(D)** Tiny red fruit in late summer is the first hint that burning bush is anticipating a seasonal change.

BURNING BUSH

## NAMED SELECTIONS

'COMPACTA': Compared to the species plant, this is a slower-growing selection that reaches 6 to 8 feet high and wide. However, it can be maintained as a 4- to 5-foot-high shrub without excessive effort. 'Compacta' is also sold as dwarf burning bush or dwarf winged euonymus.

'RUDY HAAG': This selection grows even more slowly that 'Compacta' does. You can keep this burning bush 3 to 5 feet high and wide with minimal pruning. Unless you need large plants, buy this selection if you can find it.

F

G

use for a fine plant, as long as you are aware that there are no leaves in winter to block views. If you possibly can, give burning bush species plants enough room to reach their full, glorious size.

If you've got a burning bush that has outgrown its allotted space, don't give up on it. There are two pruning choices. One is to cut the plant ruthlessly in late winter to reduce the size by about one-third. Repeat the following winter until the desired size is attained. The other option is to keep your burning bush large, but remove the lower branches to make it tree shaped, a technique known as "limbing up." This is a great way to turn an overgrown burning bush into an asset in your garden. Friends may ask you what that lovely little red tree is next autumn. To limb up your plant, make cuts judiciously, stepping back often to review your work. You won't be able to make your burning bush have a single trunk, so don't try. The goal is to expose multiple trunks while raising the canopy to expose more space beneath it. Burning bushes that only require a little trimming to maintain a desired size can likewise be pruned in late winter.

(F) The foliage of burning bush grows in attractive horizontal layers.
(G) Unless they're reaching for sunlight, burning bushes take on a naturally rounded shape.

# Butterfly Bush

*Buddleia davidii*

Also sold as *Buddleja davidii*, buddleia, orange-eyed butterfly bush

Sharubs: Showy

I
n summer, long flower spikes appear on the ends of leafy stalks. These are the neon signs of the butterfly world, advertising nectar for the taking. Each spike is actually a cluster of multiple small flowers; it is not uncommon to see more than one butterfly sharing a single flower spike. Flowerheads may droop after rain. Dozens of named selections of butterfly bushes boast varying colors of blossoms, with white, pinks, and purples the most common.

I would have called these plants "butterfly trushes." The butterfly designation is on the nose—these plants are magnets for winged beauties. But they're not really dense enough to be called bushes, and they're not substantial enough to be referred to as trees: hence, "trushes." But nobody asked me, so bushes they are. Many gardeners simply refer to these heat-loving plants by their Latin genus, *Buddleia.*

Anyone who has sun and the scrappiest amount of soil can grow a butterfly bush. Roots can be squeezed into confined situations that would be nothing less than cruel for most plants. Fertile soil is always a good thing but isn't a requirement. Avoid damp and soggy areas. Because soil pH—high or low—doesn't matter to the butterfly bush, you can grow it right beside concrete without worries of lime leaching into the soil and distressing the plant. Reflected heat from paving isn't a problem, either, as long as butterfly bushes get some water to keep them going.

Generous watering makes plants grow larger faster and yields the most flowers if sunshine is adequate. But established butterfly bushes can make do with rainfall alone in all but the driest spells. New plants set in all-day sun need water daily through their first couple of extremely hot months if rainfall is sparse. After that, reduce watering to every few days until tem-

## GETTING ACQUAINTED

Deciduous shrub (bare in winter)

6 to 12 feet high by 4 to 8 feet wide; mature plants may reach 15 feet high and wide

Showy summer flowers attract butterflies; blossom colors range from white, light pink, and lavender to deep purple and deep magenta

Rapid rate of growth

Tolerates urban conditions

All-day sun to partial shade; blooms best in sun

Any well-drained soil

Good choice for patios, entryways, vegetable gardens, low decks, butterfly gardens, growing between curbs and sidewalks, narrow spaces, city gardens, or country gardens

Pairs well with elephant ear, garlic chives, clematis, Anthony Waterer spirea, rosemary, autumn joy sedum, Heller holly, and autumn sun coneflower

Zones 5–9

Coaxing butterflies to your garden is as easy as planting a single butterfly bush. The common yellow swallowtail (*Papilio machaon*) is a frequent visitor to mine.

## PRUNING

If your butterfly bush is damaged by a late freeze or flattened by high winds, don't despair. These tough beauties are easily rejuvenated by pruning. You can cut *Buddleia davidii* back to the ground, if necessary. Feed plants after severe pruning early in the growing season with a balanced fertilizer, such as 10–10–10. Flowers form on new wood, so fresh growth will produce blossoms. In fact, giving your butterfly bush a good trim in early spring is a good way to promote flowering. Clipping spent flowers—a task known among gardeners as deadheading—will also increase flower quantities during the blooming season. Butterfly bushes bloom throughout the hot months.

## NAMED SELECTIONS

Here are some cultivars that are readily available in most areas.

'ATTRACTION': fuchsia red flowers

'BLACK KNIGHT': deep purple flowers

'BONNIE': light lavender flowers with an orange eye

'DARTMOOR': purple, fragrant flowers

'FASCINATION': lilac-pink flowers

'LOCHINCH': light blue flowers

'ORCHID BEAUTY': lavender-blue flowers

'PINK DELIGHT': true pink flowers

'ROYAL RED': rich purplish red flowers

'WHITE PROFUSION': white flowers with a yellow eye

A

B

C

peratures cool. The following hot summer, young butterfly bushes can get by with a good once-a-week soaking around the roots. Established plants desire the same, but will get by with more neglect. Always allow roots to dry out between waterings.

All-day sun is desirable for including butterfly bushes in your garden. A little shade isn't hopeless; plants will still produce a fair number of blooms. Heavy shade makes plants lean toward the sun, and both flowers and foliage are usually reduced in inadequate sunlight. There's no need to position butterfly bushes where they'll be protected from hot afternoon sun in summer. A thick layer of mulch around roots will help keep soil cool and weeds in check. Mulch also helps protect roots in winter.

Butterfly bushes have no autumn color to speak of. Blooms fizzle and leaves wither and drop. It is best to leave this plant alone through the winter months. In many parts of the South, every branch of a butterfly bush will produce new leaves in spring. In areas with cold winters, some or all of the branches may die back to the ground. Wait until the last frost to cut away dead branches. Pruning too early may encourage tender new growth to appear while there's still danger of freeze damage.

**(A)** Most butterfly bushes take on a slightly irregular form. Full sun, good drainage, and regular water yields denser crowns, but these plants will never make little lollipop trees. Pruning the branches during the growing season prevents flowering.
**(B)** Each orange-eyed flower on a cylindrical blossom spike is a potential butterfly feeding station.
**(C)** It's not unusual to spy multiple butterflies on the same plant.

# Doublefile Viburnum

*Viburnum plicatum* var. *tomentosum*

Also sold as *Viburnum tomentosum*

*Shrubs: Showy*

There's something about a doublefile viburnum in bloom that reminds me of a wedding. Snowy white flowers open as flat parasols of petals arranged around delicately embroidered centers. The profuse blossoms line the branches in double rows as if someone was determined to decorate the entire plant. This emphasizes the shrub's horizontally layered structure, making each plant appear lavishly tiered. Flowers wait to appear until May after the leaves have arrived. The result is a stunning green-and-white combination.

Doublefile viburnum demands the best soil: rich, moist, and well drained. Shrubs can adapt to soils that are poor and dry with some supplemental watering. Keep in mind that the farther south you live, the more moisture roots require, so you'll have to water a lot if your soil is naturally dry, infertile, or sandy. Doublefile viburnums grow happily in landscapes with sprinkler systems. Regular water enables these shrubs to grow in full sun, which yields the most flowers. Homeowners without automatic sprinklers would be wise to plant doublefile viburnums where they'll receive shade for several hours to half a day to help prevent wilting. However, when grown in cooler areas, such as zone 7 or at higher elevations, full sun is fine. Plants toughen up and become more drought tolerant the longer they're in place, but anticipate watering young shrubs at least through their second summer. Plant doublefile viburnums away from shallow-rooted trees such as maples and dogwoods, so the shrubs won't have to compete with tree roots for water. Avoid planting in heavy clay soils that don't drain well.

Doublefile viburnum gets big. Maturing at about 10 feet tall and wide, this shrub needs plenty of room. Plant doublefiles in groups where you

## GETTING ACQUAINTED

Deciduous shrub (bare in winter)

10 to 12 feet high and wide

Very showy white flowers cover plants in late spring after leaves appear

Moderate rate of growth

Half-day's sun; all-day sun if moisture is consistently adequate

Moist, well-drained soil

Not for urban conditions

Good choice for hedges, background plantings, or as a single specimen plant

Pairs well with lawns, Flower Carpet® rose, butterfly bush, and Siberian iris

Zones 5–8

Bountiful flowers are arranged neatly in rows on branches above the leaves of doublefile viburnum.

(A) You can't grow grass beneath a doublefile viburnum, but you can mow right up to the shrub's underskirt. Though this shrub's big show is in late spring, sporadic blossoms will appear throughout summer months.

(B) Doublefile viburnum's flowers look a lot like the blooms of lacecap hydrangeas.

(C) The foliage of doublefile viburnum has notice-able veins, as if leaves have been pleated.

need a hedge or background. Or, set a single plant where it can be admired from all sides. Doublefile viburnums are also good choices for planting in front of tall, blank walls or fences. Dig planting holes at least 5 feet away from foundations or footings so your plant will have room to grow. Avoid planting these shrubs in front of windows unless they're a good 10 or 12 feet above the ground. A doublefile that has outgrown its space can be trimmed into a tree shape by removing the lower branches to form canopy supported by a cluster of woody stems. Tree-form doublefiles resemble little kousa dogwoods. But remember, you won't be able to make the plant shorter, so be careful where you plant a doublefile viburnum.

If you don't have room for a 10-foot-wide-plant, look for a culti-var named 'Summer Snowflake'. This selection of doublefile viburnum is cultivated to stay slimmer. Though 'Summer Snowflake' can reach heights similar to the regular doublefile viburnum, these shrubs mature with spreads of 5 to 6 feet across. This means you can plant them closer together and squeeze them into narrower places. But don't be fooled by plant tags that claim 'Summer Snowflake' stays within the 4-foot-high range; plant them where they have room to grow at least twice as tall.

Doublefile viburnums have few enemies and need little pruning, provided they have adequate space. Consequently, watering young plants during their first two hot seasons or mature shrubs during a drought is the main chore. Given ideal conditions, doublefiles are completely carefree. These shrubs are naked all winter, so it's a good idea to plant them within the vicinity of evergreen plants. Some doublefile viburnums produce pretty red berries in late summer that attracts birds. However, inadequate pollination can prevent fruit production. 'Summer Snowflake' is known for bearing few berries, if any. Foliage of doublefiles turns dull to deep red in autumn before dropping.

*Rosa* Flower Carpet®

# Flower Carpet® Rose

**GETTING ACQUAINTED**

Deciduous shrub (bare in winter)

2 to 3 feet high by 3.5 feet wide

Abundant blooms in late spring to early summer, lasting for a month or more; blossom
colors vary by selection; plants continue
flowering with slightly reduced intensity
until frost

Rapid rate of growth

Tolerates urban conditions

Resistant to pests and diseases

Full sun to partial shade; blooms best in sun

Any soil that's well drained

Good choice for sunny beds, growing beside
patios or low decks, entry areas, vegetable
gardens, and courtyards

Pairs well with lawns, crepe myrtle, butterfly
bush, lantana, Kimberly Queen fern, doublefile viburnum, Siberian iris, black-eyed
Susan, purple coneflower, Queen Anne's
lace, and autumn joy sedum

Zones 5–9

A Flower Carpet® rose by any other name . . . well, it wouldn't be a Flower Carpet. This German-bred rose took twenty-five years to develop, and it is as carefree as they come. You really don't have to know anything at all about roses to be able to enjoy tremendous success with Flower Carpets.

With superior resistance to insects and diseases and an amazing ability to bloom for months, Flower Carpet roses are easy, easy, easy. If you think of them as sun-loving little shrubs, instead of *roses*, you'll find that it is really not that different from growing much of anything in your landscape. The key ingredients to success are sun, water, and once-a-year pruning and feeding. Don't let those last two tasks scare you. Though entire books are devoted to the proper care of roses, trust me, there's no great secret to trimming and fertilizing Flower Carpets. Here's what you do: In later winter, whack them back. Simply cut the stems so that they're one-third their prepruned height (but cut canes no shorter than 10 inches high). That's all there is to it. Using sharp pruners is a good idea for making clean cuts, but no special equipment is required. After you've pruned Flower Carpet roses, feed them with a time-release rose food high in potash, following the package directions. Except for watering, you're done for the year. If you get busy and don't fertilize or prune and next thing you know your plants are in bloom, it's no big deal. You can always apply the fertilizer in late summer and skip the pruning until the end of next winter. These agreeable roses will forgive you.

Though efforts are minimal, they will be rewarded with thousands of blossoms per plant. That's right, thousands. Flower Carpet roses bloom and bloom and bloom. All-day sun and a generous water supply yield the most flowers, but established plants that depend on rainfall get by okay in all but the hottest, driest spells. A little shade from western sun in the afternoon is not a bad thing, particularly in the lower zone 8 and zone 9. Flower Carpets will grow in partial sun, though flowering may be reduced. I've grown Flower Carpet roses in partial sun for years and mine open

It's hard to believe blossoms as delicately colored as those of 'Appleblossom' Flower Carpet roses are could be so easy and heat-proof. A new 'Amber' selection will be available soon.

A

B

C

**(A)** Flower Carpet roses are unbelievably prolific bloomers. This one is simply called 'Pink'. *Photo courtesy of Ferguson Caras LLC*

**(B)** You can grow Flower Carpet roses in large containers set in the sun. Provide a little extra water for pot-grown roses. *Photo courtesy of Ferguson Caras LLC*

**(C)** Trim Flower Carpet roses back in late winter to get the most flowers. *Photo courtesy of Ferguson Caras LLC*

## FLOWER CARPET® CHOICES

'Appleblossom': also sold as Noamel; pastel pink, double, *photo courtesy of Ferguson Caras LLC*

'Coral': also sold as Noala; coral pink, semi-double, *photo courtesy of Ferguson Caras LLC*

'Coral', single, *photo courtesy of Ferguson Caras LLC*

'Pink': also sold as Noatraum; rich hot pink, double

'Red': also sold as Noare; deep red, single, *photo courtesy of Ferguson Caras LLC*

'Scarlet': also sold as NOA83100; bright scarlet red, double, *photo courtesy of Ferguson Caras LLC*

'White': also sold as Noaschnee; snowy white, *photo courtesy of Ferguson Caras LLC*

'Yellow': also sold as Noalesa; butter yellow, *photo courtesy of Ferguson Caras LLC*

plenty of flowers, though I notice that the Flower Carpet roses grown in a full sun in a local park surpass the plentiful mark. Those shrubs are completely covered with blossoms from head to toe. They tend to keep blooming longer, too, but maybe that's because I'm too lazy to fertilize or water and haven't chopped my roses back in years. (Note to self: Whack back the Flower Carpets this spring.)

Avoid planting these roses in dense shade, which will make plants scraggly and flowerless. A good six hours of direct sun per day is ideal. Any soil that drains well will do, though naturally the good stuff makes plants happy. Amend planting holes with a dollop or two of compost and apply the little packet of fertilizer that usually comes with each Flower Carpet rose. Water new plants thoroughly by slowly soaking the soil around the roots. Be generous with water during hot months, especially during the plant's first year in your landscape.

Flower Carpet roses are advertised as ground-cover roses because they grow wider than they do tall. This description also comes from the fact that Flower Carpets bear leaves and blossoms all over—right to the ground—unlike many roses that are bare sticks for the first foot or so of trunk. But use these plants in the landscape as you would a modest-sized shrub. Flower Carpets look great massed together; fill an entire sunny bed with them. Or, grow them in front of taller shrubs to add a lower layer of color to the composition—you'll look quite the pro. You can also grow a single Flower Carpet rose as a specimen where it can be admired from all sides. These plants are excellent for growing beside your favorite summer outdoor spots. Border a patio or low deck, set them beside steps, or add them to your vegetable garden for color. If there's ample sun, grow Flower Carpet roses near your front door to welcome guests and guide them to the entry you really want them to use. Open areas with good air circulation are better for any roses than beds confined by solid walls, as poor air circulation may promote powdery mildew.

# Glossy Abelia

*Abelia* x *grandiflora*

Also sold as abelia

**G**row glossy abelia where azaleas would bite the dust. These tough shrubs love full sun and poor soil and even thrive beside paving—reflected heat doesn't faze them in the least. Humidity is no problem, and few shrubs tolerate drought the way glossy abelia does. Though glossy abelia's multitudes of little white flowers are too modest to be called spectacular, they do bloom from early summer right through the dog days and into autumn, attracting beaucoup butterflies all the while.

This shrub's airy, arching branches give the garden a casual appearance. Each branch is dense with twigs and tiny leaves. The foliage of glossy abelia is shiny; that's where the glossy part of its name comes from. Leaves are green with a maroon tint in summer and turn bronzy when tempera-

tures cool. The farther south you live, the more leaves your glossy abelia will keep throughout the winter months. In colder areas that regularly experience freezing temperatures, plants may shed foliage altogether. New leaves are reddish when they first appear in spring.

Water young glossy abelia shrubs well upon planting and give them a drink every now and then to help them through the first summer. After that, let nature take it from there. (However, if you're eager for quick growth, it is okay to water regularly as long as your soil drains well.) Though glossy abelia can adapt to some shade, shrubs that don't receive enough sunlight eventually become top-heavy, with most of the foliage borne on bare, spindly stems. You'll enjoy prettier plants if you grow them in sunny spots in your garden. All-day sun is fine, and there's no need to protect plants from western rays. Avoid areas that stay damp. Sunny, dry slopes cry out for this heat-loving, drought-tolerant shrub.

Glossy abelia can go for years without pruning, but you may remove stalks that have few leaves to encourage fresh growth. This will result

**GETTING ACQUAINTED**

Semi-deciduous shrub

4 to 6 feet high and wide

Little flowers attract butterflies in summer. Plants have tiny leaves and loose, airy forms.

Rapid rate of growth

Drought and heat tolerant

Resistant to pests and disease

All-day sun to mostly sunny

Any soil that's well drained

Good choice for informal hedges, dry slopes, good-sized beds beside patios, framing high porches and low decks, parking areas, and hot spots where nothing but weeds are growing

Pairs well with purple coneflower, black-eyed Susan, rosemary, autumn joy sedum, autumn sun coneflower, Mexican bush sage, garlic chives, crepe myrtle, and lantana

Zones 5–9

Glossy abelia is best grown in groups, so don't buy fewer than three of these plants. It's preferable to purchase more. Except for dwarf varieties, shrubs may be leggy at the bottom, so planting them on a slope or behind a low wall emphasizes the arching branches instead of leafless lower stems. Full sun yields the leafiest shrubs.

## NAMED SELECTIONS

'EDWARD GOUCHER': about 4 feet high; pink flowers
   in summer and well into autumn
'PROSTRATA': only 2 feet high; white blooms
'SHERWOOD': about 4 feet high; pale pink blooms;
   foliage turns purplish in winter

## BUDGET MINDED

If you're in need of a lot of shrubs, consider glossy abelia.
Not only does this plant grow quickly, but its tolerance of
heat and drought also means that glossy abelia has a
good survival rate despite summer heat.

## ATTRACTING BUTTERFLIES

Though the flowers of glossy abelia are small,
they attract multitudes of butterflies.

Eastern black swallowtail
(*Papilio polyxenes*)

Common yellow swallow-
tail (*Papilio machaon*)

Cloudless sulfur (*Phoebis
sennae*)

in more flowers and foliage. Don't shear plants to shape
them. Instead, reach inside shrubs and remove thick, old,
gray-barked stems by hand-cutting them at their base. Use
the same technique if you need to reduce the size of glossy
abelia, and you'll be able to preserve its naturally airy form.
To rejuvenate aged, truly overgrown plants, cut them back
to uneven clumps about 2 feet tall late in winter to prompt
fresh, arching growth (don't do this regularly). You'll miss
a season of flowers following severe pruning. It's important
to resist the urge to shape glossy abelia into boxes or balls
because you'll end up with collections of woody sticks with
few leaves or flowers.

Excluding dwarf selections, unpruned glossy abelia can
top 6 feet in height, so keep these shrubs away from low
windows. Instead, grow them as a background, informal
hedge, or as a buffer to screen unwanted views. Glossy abelia
is also attractive when planted at the foot of a high porch or
low deck, beside stone walls or paving, or when grown near
plants that remain dark green all year. Consider planting a
row of these shrubs instead of building a fence. You can leave
an opening in the row to add an arch or a gate mounted on a
pair of posts to dress up your living fence.

# Korean Spice Viburnum

*Viburnum carlesii*

Also sold as Koreanspice bush

I used to be personally acquainted with a Korean spice viburnum that lived in my neighborhood, but new owners cut the thing down in late summer, not knowing what the shrub had in store for them in spring. Had they ever caught one whiff of the fragrance that perfumes the air when Korean spice viburnum blooms, I've no doubt that the saw would have been put away unused.

The sturdy blossoms of this old-fashioned shrub are ideal for clipping to bring inside and fill your home with the scent of spring. The fragrance is heady but not offensive; no one dislikes it. Sweet-smelling flowers are the main reason to plant a Korean spice viburnum, and they're reason enough. Bright pink buds appear in clusters in early spring. By the time they open as fragrant balls of blooms, leaves are starting to unfurl on the branches, too. Flowers are white tinged with pink.

This old garden favorite is dull green in summer. It turns bright scarlet in autumn in cold regions, but reddish autumn color in the South is not usually noteworthy. The stiff branches are bare in winter, so position shrubs where they won't be missed when leaves are down. Because Korean spice viburnum is quite adaptable with regard to its space and sun requirements, you can tuck one or two unobtrusively into the landscape. You'll enjoy the flowers and the fragrance for two weeks or more in spring and then forget about this shrub the rest of the year. It is a good idea to plant one where you'll pass it daily to maximize its value in spring.

Korean spice viburnum gets large, about 6 to 8 feet high and wide. When grown in all-day sun, shrubs are full and round. When grown in the shade, they assume irregular but pleasant forms as they adapt to fill

## GETTING ACQUAINTED

Deciduous shrub (bare in winter)

6 to 8 feet high and wide in sun; requires less room in shade

In spring, pink buds open to white blooms that have an incredibly lovely fragrance

Slow rate of growth

Drought resistant

Partial sun to all-day sun

Slightly acidic, well-drained soil

Good choice for natural areas, background plantings, tucking into landscapes near front or back doors

Pairs well with nandina, Siberian iris, pansies, and spring bulbs

Zones 5–8

Flowers cut from Korean spice viburnum make delightful gifts for friends and neighbors. They'll love the fragrance.

the available space and seek what sunshine they can get. Homeowners in zones 7 and northward can grow plants in full or partial sun. Korean spice viburnums grown in zone 8 landscapes, where summers are long and hot, are better suited for partial sun instead of all-day sun. Morning sun is preferable over blazing afternoon sun from the west, which can scorch leaves in July or August. Because Korean spice viburnum flowers before most hardwood trees have leaves, it is not challenging to plant these shrubs where they'll receive winter sun and midsummer shade.

Established plants withstand drought well. The farther south you live and the more sun your Korean spice viburnum receives, the more likely it is that you'll need to water when the weather is hot and dry. Shrubs grown in full sun can be lightly pruned occasionally to encourage a rounded shape, but let plants in the shade find their own form. Autumn is the best time to add Korean spice viburnum to your landscape. Buy shrubs grown on their own rootstock (not grafted) to get the true old-fashioned species plant with the original, amazing fragrance.

(A) Summer foliage of Korean spice viburnum is a dull gray-green. In cold climates, autumn color is outstanding, but it is rarely noticeable in the South.
(B) The dark pink buds of Korean spice viburnum appear like spiky balls in early spring.
(C) The flowers themselves are paler than the buds. White petals are barely blushed with pink. Fortunately, you can enjoy the pink buds and perfumed flowers together for a while.

# Winter Jasmine

*Jasminum nudiflorum*

Also sold as January jasmine, hardy jasmine

Winter jasmine is one stubborn plant, which makes it very easy to grow. A large, arching, durable shrub, winter jasmine thrives in any kind of soil except very wet. Poor, dry soil—the kind you find on hillsides—is no deterrent. In fact, such bleak conditions are just fine for growing winter jasmine. This tough plant's arching shape spills attractively down banks and over the tops of retaining walls, so it is an ideal choice for slopes. All-day sun is best, though partial shade is tolerated, especially if sun can reach winter jasmine from December to February or March.

As its name implies, winter jasmine obstinately insists on blooming in winter. The least little warm spell will cause small yellow flowers to pop open along the slender stems. The return of cold weather usually puts a temporary stop to flowering. Then, along comes a sunny day or two and winter jasmine stubbornly blooms a little more. The result is a scattered show of cheerful yellow flowers throughout winter and into spring. In mild years when winter jasmine blooms uninterrupted by cold snaps, it puts on a more dramatic display. Though this shrub is bare of leaves all winter, its arched stems stay green. The buttery flowers appear before leaves do, showing off nicely along the green stems. This habit makes the plant's species name, *nudiflorum*, easy to remember: Winter jasmine is a shrub that flowers in the nude.

The most challenging aspect of growing winter jasmine in your landscape is finding enough room for it. Each plant forms a mound that can get as large as 7 feet across. Clusters grow thickly due to branches that root wherever they come into contact with moist soil. Because branches arch and lean over, this shrub doesn't get much higher than 4 feet, but its wide spread eats up a lot of

**GETTING ACQUAINTED**

Deciduous shrub (bare in winter)

4 feet high by 7 feet wide

Extremely early yellow flowers decorate green arching stems from late winter through early spring

Rapid rate of growth

Resistant to drought, insects, and disease

All-day sun to mostly sunny

Any soil except wet

Suitable for urban conditions if space permits

Good choice for slopes, growing at the top of retaining walls, grouping together as large masses

Pairs well with nandina, burning bush, glossy abelia, crepe myrtle, and Mexican bush sage, but provide ample room to avoid crowding other plants

Zones 6–10

The tubular yellow flowers of winter jasmine are about 1 inch long. They perch along square, green stems before leaves appear.

You can grow winter jasmine in a good-sized planter to add color during the cool months.

## THE OTHER JASMINE

Winter jasmine is closely related to Florida jasmine (*Jasminum floridum*), another arching shrub that bears small yellow flowers. But Florida jasmine thrives in rare-frost and frost-free areas and keeps its leaves all year. It also gets even larger than winter jasmine. A single Florida jasmine can easily grow 10 feet high and 15 feet across. Like winter jasmine, its cousin thrives in full sun but will grow in partial shade. Poor, dry soil is not a problem, and this jasmine is also ideal for slopes. Florida jasmine will suffer cold damage and is likely to die in areas where winter freezes are a regular occurrence. It is best limited to landscapes in lower zone 8 and southward.

The best way to tell these two shrubby jasmines apart when they're both cute little things growing in nursery containers is to look at their leaf arrangement. The triplet foliage of winter jasmine grows on little stems that are across from each other on the branch; each leaf stem is directly opposite another. Florida jasmine's leaf stems zigzag their way up the branch in alternating fashion. Florida jasmine may be sold as flowering jasmine or showy jasmine.

space. The large size is a useful characteristic if you've got a lot of ground to cover; just make sure to think things through before you start sticking winter jasmine in the ground. Except for the occasional removal of a few wayward branches, you really can't control the size of such a resolute plant by pruning.

Rather, pruning is a task that should be limited to every four years or so. That's when you should show no mercy. Wait until after flowering ceases and cut winter jasmine back hard. Remove long sprays, leaving trimmed branches between 1 and 2 feet in length. (It is best to stagger cuts at different lengths to avoid the crew-cut look and to encourage stems to arch.) Severe pruning will promote fresh growth, giving plants new life. By whacking winter jasmine back right after it blooms, you'll give shrubs ample time to grow new shoots that will bear flowers the following year. Such reinvigorating pruning is preferable to cutting the ends of sprays off at the same level. You'll often see this unfortunate approach taken by

A

B

homeowners who realize that their winter jasmine has completely hidden an attractive retaining wall. It is an ill-advised technique that's contrary to winter jasmine's graceful tumbling shape. It also encourages a mass of not-so-pretty twiggy growth along the cut line.

Shiny green foliage covers winter jasmine from spring through autumn, when it fades away without any noticeable autumn color. The leaves grow in little trios, filling out the shrub's shape and adding a delicate texture that contrasts nicely with rough stone walls or boulders. Established plants rarely need supplemental watering, even during drought conditions.

(A) Winter jasmine is a good choice for cascading over a retaining wall.
(B) The delicately small foliage of winter jasmine adds fine texture to vertical surfaces from spring until winter.

# Evergreen Shrubs

# Heller Holly

*Ilex crenata* 'Helleri'

Also sold as Heller Japanese holly

Shrubs: Evergreen

Heller holly is one of those plants that you can easily walk right past at the garden center. After all, when there are so many showy plants from which to choose, who wants to buy a little green shrub that doesn't even bloom? You should. And not just one—you ought to buy a whole bunch of them.

Despite its lack of pizzazz, Heller holly is a landscaping workhorse. It is a sandwich shrub, a modest green plant that's equally useful growing behind bright bedding plants and in front of taller shrubs. Colorful flowers become more noticeable when they're showcased against plain Jane plants like Heller hollies. These low shrubs never clash with house colors, making them ideal for including in foundation plantings. Heller hollies stay green year-round, so their presence is not limited by the seasons.

This shrub's broad, mounding shape is a big plus, too. You can plant Heller hollies in front of low windows without worrying about blocking views. You can also grow these short, useful shrubs to skirt leggier plants such as nandina or butterfly bush. Or, add a group of Hellers in front of hedges or beds of taller shrubs for a layered effect. Fill a bed with these little shrubs while leaving an empty niche for flowers, and you'll have a great spot to add seasonal color with

maximum impact. Heller holly's spreading habit makes it a fine filler for raised planters, empty spots beside steps, and beds surrounding patios, low decks, and porches.

Its compact size and rate of growth are closely related: Heller holly stays low and grows slowly. Though a single plant may eventually grow to be 6 feet wide, it could take a decade to do it. You can usually count on Heller hollies to grow about 3 feet tall and wide with no pruning required.

### GETTING ACQUAINTED

Evergreen shrub

3 to 4 feet high by 3 to 6 feet wide

This shrub is known for its dense, compact form and year-round greenery

All-day sun to partial shade

Moist, fertile soil that's well drained; not for wet or alkaline soil

Needs little to no pruning

Good choice for foundation planting, framing annual beds, skirting taller shrubs, planting in front of low windows, growing beside patios, low decks, and porches, and filling raised beds and planters

Pairs well with butterfly bush, nandina, sun-loving seasonal flowers, lawns, Anthony Waterer spirea, creeping phlox, candytuft, garlic chives, and autumn joy sedum

Zones 6–8

Let plants grow together to form a mass of greenery. They'll look fresh and green in every season.

## CHINESE HOLLY

If you're accustomed to thinking of holly as a plant with large, prickly leaves, think again. That spiny-leafed plant is Chinese holly (*Ilex cornuta*), and it is just one type of holly. Heller holly belongs to the Japanese side of the family. Japanese hollies are known for small evergreen leaves and dense growth.

## MASS PLANTING

The best way to use Heller hollies in your landscape is to grow them in a mass. Plan ahead to let plants grow together to form a solid sea of green. The result is a touch of formality without the stuffiness—or effort—of tightly clipped shrubs.

To grow a mass, start by setting new plants in a bed using a triangular spacing pattern. First, align the front row of plants to repeat the shape of the edge of the bed. Set the next row of plants in a staggered manner so they're positioned between the front plants, and so forth. This creates a checkerboard of plants that can grow to fill in the entire bed much more quickly and effectively than lined-up rows of plants ever could.

*Stagger young Heller hollies to fill beds faster.*

As your bed of Heller hollies grow and begin to touch one another, resist the temptation to shear each shrub into distinctively separate plants. Separating the plants ruins the effect of the mass. What's the point of such shearing, anyway—to see the mulch between the plants? Heller hollies are valuable and attractive when grown together as a sweep of greenery. Buy at least seven of these shrubs and preferably more.

A

B

SHRUBS: EVERGREEN

D

E

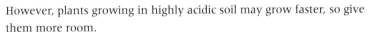

C

However, plants growing in highly acidic soil may grow faster, so give them more room.

Heller holly thrives in all-day sun or partial shade. Once plants are established, they're easy. But a little effort is needed to assure a continued state of contentment. Most of the effort comes up front at planting time. Heller hollies won't tolerate wet feet—plants stranded in wet soil will quickly die. This makes it important to enrich your soil prior to sticking Heller hollies into the ground. Work organic matter into the soil to add nutrients and improve drainage. (If you can, till composted organic matter into the entire bed where these hollies will be planted, instead of just mixing the amendments into individual holes.) If your soil is heavy clay, it's probably a good idea to build a raised bed to make sure the water will drain away from roots. Gentle slopes and beds behind retaining walls are naturally likely to drain well, making them good spots for growing Heller hollies.

That's not to say that dry conditions are the answer, either. Heller hollies want moist soil with good drainage. They'll need supplemental watering during periods of drought. This shrub's stiff, twiggy little branches and tiny leaves means that it never wilts, so you can't count on that usual clue to alert you to the fact that your Heller hollies need additional water. It is up to you to recognize a drought and turn on the sprinklers or uncoil the hose. If a Heller holly is too wet or too dry, it will up and die on you with no warning at all.

Scared away from growing this plant? Don't be. The older plants are, the more drought tolerant they become. Your efforts at planting time will be rewarded with years of enjoying a tidy sweep of low-maintenance greenery. So do the work when you dig the hole, and save yourself years of pruning by choosing this compact shrub.

(A) Heller holly is a good ingredient in the recipe for a great landscape. This short shrub is ideal for growing beside steps or beneath low windows.
(B) While no one but a fellow plant person is likely to specifically admire your Heller hollies, everyone will notice the professional look of your landscape.
(C) Heller holly's branching structure is naturally horizontal, so plants grow out more than they do up.
(D) Heller holly makes a tidy frame for spots of seasonal color, such as this patch of tulips.
(E) In ideal growing conditions, Heller hollies eventually grow to form mounding shrubs 3 to 4 feet high.

*Nandina domestica*

Also sold as heavenly bamboo

# Nandina

**GETTING ACQUAINTED**

Evergreen shrub

4 to 6 feet high by 2 to 3 feet wide

Ornamental red berries are showy in winter; feathery foliage arranged in layers is present year-round

Moderate to slow rate of growth

Tolerates heat, cold, and drought

Resistant to insects and disease

Long-lived and hard to kill

Produces young plants; may be invasive in frost-free areas

Full sun to partial shade

Any soil that's well drained

Prune occasionally to control height and encourage full, bushy form

Good choice for narrow spaces, parking areas, patios, hedges, foundation plantings, backgrounds in seasonal flowerbeds

Pairs well with Heller holly, liriope, bridalwreath spirea, Anthony Waterer spirea, autumn joy sedum, black-eyed Susan, candytuft, bronze fennel, garlic chives, Siberian iris, creeping phlox, lantana, winter jasmine and elephant ear

Zones 7–10

Not only are nandinas useful in the landscape, they're also valuable for school projects and architectural models: Pluck the berries from branched twigs and you've got perfect miniature trees.

If only all plants were as tough as nandina. I've seen it dug up during construction, chucked in the corner of the yard with no soil cover and no water, replanted months later, chopped to the ground to get rid of leggy old stems, only to come back in fine form. This is one durable plant. When homeowners ask me about transplanting old shrubs in an effort to cut costs when renovating a landscape, I rarely approve if they're not going to do the digging themselves. The labor cost of relocating plants that may not survive the process is frequently higher than the price of new, healthy plants. But nandinas are a different story. The survival rate of transplanted nandinas is so high that it seems criminal to pitch these plants instead of moving them to a new spot.

Not only is nandina resilient, it's attractive as well. The foliage grows in delicate layers, giving plants a lacy look. Nandina is evergreen, so it provides a year-round presence in the landscape. Foliage often turns red, bronze, or wine colored after a cold snap in autumn; new layers of fresh leaves in spring may start off in similar hues. Though creamy spring flowers aren't particularly showy, they yield large sprays of berries that turn brilliant red in winter. The fruit would be eye-catching any time of year, but coming as it does during the cold months when much of the landscape is brown or gray, the bright bounty is even more conspicuous. Berries last on plants into spring.

Nandina can live for generations. Though longevity is a good thing, it has given a good plant a bad name. Nandinas that have long been growing in the same location often take on a spindly appearance that's quite unattractive. One reason for the gawky look is that nandinas originally

With lacy foliage on branches that never go bare, nandina is ideal for planting to skirt foundations and porches.

## NANDINA MAKEOVERS

### TRANSPLANTING

If a leggy nandina isn't getting at least a half-day's sun, dig it up and move it to a sunnier spot. You can do this any time of year. Use a sharp-bladed shovel to cut a circle around the plant that's at least 1 foot beyond trunks on all sides. Once you've gotten the rootball out of the ground, it's simply a matter of hauling it to its new home and sticking it in a new hole. A spot with all-day sun is best. Water thoroughly to help the plant adjust. Then, prune as described below. You'll be amazed at the transformation from a gawky flamingo of a plant (all leg, no fluff) to a bushy beauty.

### SEVERE PRUNING

You'll need to severely prune a nandina if it is overgrown and woody. The technique is the same whether the sunlight is adequate and the shrub has merely been neglected or if nandina has just been moved to a sunnier location. First, randomly select a third of the stalks, or canes, throughout the plant. Cut these to within inches of the ground. Next, select another third of the remaining canes, and remove two-thirds of their height. Don't worry that you're

*This durable shrub can grow with no attention at all, but occasional pruning every few years is recommended to keep nandina bushy and full.*

cutting off all the leaves. They'll grow back. For the rest of the stalks, prune to remove one-third of the height, so that these canes now stand at two-thirds of their original height.

This stair-step pruning technique is easy to do—don't cheat and flattop your plant. Nandina doesn't produce lateral branches, so you must cut canes at different levels throughout the plants to make shrubs full and bushy. After severe pruning, you won't get berries for at least one winter, maybe two. You also won't need to cut your nandina for many years. When plants get gawky again, trim them in a modified stair-step manner, described at right.

### OCCASIONAL PRUNING

You don't need as heavy a hand when it comes to pruning nandina occasionally to maintain it. Pruning this plant is not an annual chore. In fact, years should pass between trimmings. You'll know it is time to prune when you notice your nandina getting leggy and woody instead of fluffy with foliage.

The difference between occasional pruning and severe pruning is that none of the stalks are cut to the ground during occasional pruning. Instead, a third of randomly selected stalks are not cut at all, another third has one-third of their current height removed, and the remaining third of stalks get two-thirds of their height cut away. Make sure that the stalks pruned to different heights and the uncut stalks are distributed randomly throughout the plant for a scattered stair-step effect. This will result in a leafy, bushy plant.

Remember, if you prune too often, you'll never get to enjoy berries. Though you can trim these shrubs any time of year, winter is a good time for pruning nandina because cut berries are great for using in long-lasting holiday arrangements indoors and out.

A

B

(A) The outer sprays of nandina foliage often turn wine-red in winter.

(B) Nandina tolerates confined root conditions, enabling you to add greenery and color where most plants won't grow.

(C) Nandina's height makes it a perfect choice for the back row of layered planting compositions.

## NAMED SELECTIONS

'AUTROPURPUREA NANA': also sold as 'Nana Purpurea' or 'Nana'; 12 inches high; leaves often distorted and unattractive

'GULFSTREAM': naturally fluffy at just 4 feet high; foliage turns red to bronze after the first cold snap; no flowers or berries

'LOWBOY': stays about 3 feet high; leaves turn red in autumn; produces flowers and berries

HARBOR BELLE®: also sold as 'Jaytee'; maximum height of 2 feet; produces flowers and berries; new growth pinkish in spring

C

SHRUBS: EVERGREEN

D

E

F

planted in the sun can end up in the shade many years later when trees mature. Dense shade makes these shrubs grow woody and leggy with sparse foliage. Another reason for the decline in appearance is that nandinas—easy to grow and easy to forget about—are commonly neglected. After years without pruning, nandina grows tall canes that are barren except for tufts of foliage at the tops. If that's your impression of nandina, it's little wonder if you dislike it. But take a second look. Nandina that receives adequate sunlight and has been properly pruned is a totally different creature. Fortunately, it's an easy plant to reclaim (see page 77).

The value of nandina in the landscape is hard to beat. This shrub pairs well with any plant that doesn't mind dry soil and which thrives in all-day sun to partial shade. Nandina is a particularly useful shrub for providing winter interest to beds of seasonal flowers that disappear in winter. It also helps distract attention from deciduous plants that are bare during cold months. With adaptable roots that don't mind being confined, an upright form, and soft foliage that won't scratch cars or people, nandina is great for tucking into narrow spaces. Use it to fill empty corners or squeeze it beside driveways. Include it in foundation planting, grow it as a hedge, or plant it in masses in beds. Nandina is a decorative shrub that's as useful as it is durable.

(D) Cut entire sprays of nandina berries for use in Christmas decorations. They'll hold their color for a month or more after cutting.

(E) Nandina berries have long been a traditional decoration in Southern cemeteries.

(F) Occasionally, you can find yellow-berried nandina (Nandina domestica var. leucocarpa) for sale.

*Rosmarinus officinalis*

# Rosemary

S ure, it is a culinary herb, but a plant as pretty, tough, and fragrant
as rosemary deserves better than to be limited to the herb garden.
Some upright varieties grow 6 to 7 feet high and over 4 feet wide,
claiming shrub status in the landscape. The gray-green foliage is present
year-round, covering stems like fluffy spruce needles. Rosemary lives
from three to ten years. All-day sun and well-drained soil produce the

healthiest, longest-lived plants.
Six to eight hours of sunlight is
ideal. Brutal, hot afternoon sun
is no problem. Plenty of sun and
a strategy for providing moisture
without keeping roots wet for long
is the key to growing rosemary
successfully.

Rosemary doesn't need
much water, so don't overwater
plants, even young ones. Always
poke a finger in the soil to check
the moisture before watering—it is
best to let roots dry out completely
between waterings. Plant rosemary
in spots that drain well, such as
sandy or rocky beds, slopes, and
raised beds or planters. As long
as water drains away from roots,
rosemary doesn't mind confined
spaces. This evergreen is unfazed
by reflected heat from paving, so
you can plant it in alongside walkways, in beds surrounded by patios, and
tucked into crevices within paving. Rosemary also thrives at the top of
retaining walls. In acid soil, occasional light applications of lime will help
sweeten the soil, raising the pH to rosemary's liking.

Rosemary grows in dense, spiky clumps. Though narrow gray-green
leaves are stiff, they're so numerous that the plant has a fuzzy look to it.
This fine texture makes a nice contrast with large, coarse-textured stone-
work or boulders. Small flowers open during warm months, decorating
rosemary branches with bits of blue or violet. A few varieties offer pink or

Tall selections of rosemary make good filler
between large perennials, such as Mexican bush
sage, and smaller ones, such as garlic chives.

A

B

white flowers. Butterflies are attracted to the tiny blossoms, which are a nectar source for several species. Bees like the blooms, too.

To keep rosemary vigorous and full, pinch it back regularly. Always remove less than a quarter of the plant, maximum, when pinching or pruning this herb. Use the aromatic clippings in cooking, herbal baths, or root them in water or sand to start new plants. There's no need to shear rosemary unless you're aiming for a certain shape, such a little pyramid or lollipop topiary. Remove a few woody stems whenever branches seem to lose vitality with age. New shoots will add fresh greenery to plants.

**(A)** Shorter rosemary selections are useful anywhere you've got sun and well-drained soil. Shrubs that have leggy bases, such as butterfly bush, are improved in appearance when skirted with shorter selections of rosemary.
**(B)** Rosemary that's pinched back regularly grows bushy and full, like this one hugging the steps at left.

### FLAT AND FEATHERY SELECTIONS

Prostrate rosemary grows out, not up. This form of the plant is useful as a groundcover. Use it to cascade over retaining walls, or surround birdbaths or sculpture in sunny spots. You can also add prostrate rosemary to fill gaps left in paving. With its sprawling form and preference for dry roots, prostrate rosemary is an excellent choice for growing on slopes where water naturally drains downhill away from roots. You can also include prostrate rosemary in hanging baskets, planters, and large containers.

Named selections of prostrate rosemary include 'Prostratus', Irene®, 'Huntington Carpet', and 'Mrs. Howard's Creeping'. The Santa Barbara rosemary (also sold as 'Lockwood de Forest') grows just 2 feet high, but a single plant may grow 8 feet across. In general, prostrate rosemary is more sensitive to cold than upright selections. Of the prostrate varieties, 'Dancing Waters' gets the best marks for cold hardiness.

*Santa Barbara rosemary stays low and trails.*

### UPRIGHT ROSEMARY SELECTIONS

'TUSCAN BLUE': abundant dark blue flowers; larger blossoms than species; 6 to 7 feet high
'MAJORCA PINK': pink blossoms; 3 to 5 feet high
'ALBUS': white flowers; 3 feet high
'ARP': cold-hardy to -10°F; blue flowers; 4 feet high
'HILL HARDY': also sold as 'Madeline Hill' or 'Hardy Hill'; cold-hardy to 0°F and maybe a little below; blue flowers; 3 to 5 feet high

A

C

B

(A) Fat little needles release rosemary's trademark scent and flavor when crushed. Foliage is gray-green all year.

(B) The tiny flowers of rosemary range in color from sky-blue to lavender to deep blue. The blossoms attract butterflies.

(C) As long as you choose a container that drains well, you can grow rosemary in a pot.

(D) Prostrate rosemary can be grown as a ground-cover or as a weeping plant along the face of retaining walls, planters, and containers.

D

E

F

To enjoy rosemary's fragrance, plant it beside gates, steps, doors, and walkways. If you brush against it, the plant will release more of the aroma. Rosemary grows well in containers if the planting mix is light enough to ensure good drainage. Potted rosemary may be preferable in areas that regularly experience hard freezes in the winter, as containers can easily be brought inside. Most selections of rosemary will be damaged or killed when temperatures dip to 30°F. However, a cultivar named 'Arp' has earned a reputation for surviving at -10°F and 'Hill Hardy' tolerates cold snaps down to 0°F.

In semi-tropical areas, the problem may be seasonal rainfall, not temperature. Rosemary grown in climates that see periods of prolonged rain may require temporary shelter to keep roots from becoming waterlogged. Good air circulation is important for keeping rosemary healthy, so don't plant it in spots sequestered from breezes.

(E) Rosemary adds soothing greenery to planting compositions, making colorful plants more noticeable.
(F) Rosemary can be trained around hoops to form topiaries or grown on a single stalk with clipped foliage, like a little poodle tree.
*Designer Randy McManus, Chapel Hill, North Carolina*

Trees

# Showy Trees

# Crepe Myrtle

*Lagerstroemia indica*

May be sold as crape myrtle
or crapemyrtle

Just as the twin icons of Southern gardening, the azalea and the camellia, are Asian imports, so is our beloved crepe myrtle. These pretty trees get left off lists of approved native plants by well-meaning streetscaping committees with good reason—they're not native. Nonetheless, crepe myrtles have definitely earned their keep in the Southern landscape since their introduction to Charleston, South Carolina, in 1790 by a visiting French botanist.

With fabulous colorful blooms and a sun- and heat-loving, drought-tolerant constitution that can only be described as Southern, the crepe myrtle is a worthy exotic. Crepe myrtles celebrate summer with profuse plumes of flowers that come in a variety of colors, including white, lavender, and every shade of pink from a pale blush to vibrant watermelon to red, with many hues in between. Blossoms are delicately crinkled like crepe paper. A crepe myrtle in full bloom is guaranteed to turn heads.

Not only can crepe myrtles take hot sun, they demand it. Plant yours in all-day sun for best results; mostly sunny spots are suitable, too. Crepe myrtles grown in the shade of larger trees have fewer blossoms and will eventually lean toward the sun. Avoid planting these trees squashed up against fences, walls, and other plants. Good air flow around all sides of a crepe myrtle is the best defense against powdery mildew, an unsightly fungus that coats leaves with gray and distorts new growth. (For an organic treatment of powdery mildew, see the bee balm section.)

Crepe myrtles don't care about soil pH, so pretty much any Southerner can grow them. In fact, any soil is fine as long as it isn't consistently wet.

**GETTING ACQUAINTED**

Deciduous tree (bare in winter)

20 to 30 feet tall by 15 to 20 foot wide

Usually grown as a multiple-trunked tree (available as single-trunked "standards" but these trunks don't always grow straight)

Large summer blossoms open in varying shades of white, pink, purple, and red

Rapid rate of growth

Roots will not harm paving

All-day sun to mostly sunny

Any soil except wet

Good choice for planting along streets, driveways, in parking areas and entry gardens, and on slopes

Pairs well with black-eyed Susan, purple coneflower, lilac chaste-tree, glossy abelia, rosemary, garlic chives, and liriope

Zones 7–9

*Trees: Showy*

Crepe myrtles grown in full sun develop the best autumn color.

## SCULPTURE VERSUS TORTURE

Take your pick. Your crepe myrtle can show off as a living piece of sculpture in winter, featuring trunks that become more muscular and sleek from peeled bark as they age. Or, you can whack away at your tree and have a bunch of ugly sticks to look at throughout the cold months. Choose sculpture over torture and leave your crepe myrtle unpruned. You'll be rewarded with a healthy, attractive tree with strong branches.

*Living sculpture*

*Tree torture*

Crepe myrtles that are cut each year develop unsightly knots in their trunks resembling fists. As trees attempt to recover from the vicious pruning, they send out multiple sprouts from each knot. True, each sprout produces blooms, but the new growth is so lanky that it can't support the weight of blossoms, especially when they're wet. Crepe myrtles that droop under the weight of their own flowers after a summer rainstorm are trees that were pruned the autumn or winter before. The truth is, no pruning is needed at all. Just leave your crepe myrtles alone during the cold months, trim away suckers during the growing season, and you'll enjoy beautiful trees for years to come.

I'm convinced that the current cut-your-crepe mentality is the work of maintenance companies who need to justify their existence during slow winter months. When one homeowner cuts his crepe myrtles, the neighbors aren't far behind. But remember, there's no need to jump off the crepe myrtle cliff just because everyone else is.

## BENIGN NEGLECT

Crepe myrtles are so easy to grow that gardeners sometimes invent things to do to them just to feel needed. But unless a crepe myrtle is newly planted or is stressed by an extreme drought, there's no need to water. In fact, too much water is bad for your tree. Crepe myrtles rarely need fertilizer, and none containing nitrogen should ever be applied after spring. Watering, fertilizing, and pruning trees in autumn encourages new growth at the wrong time of year, increasing chances of freeze damage. So leave your crepe myrtle alone and find some pickier plant to bother.

## SOOTY MOLD

If the leaves of your crepe myrtle are covered with a black substance, don't worry, it won't hurt the tree and it won't affect next year's leaves or flowers. The black stuff is sooty mold and it grows on honeydew, the sweetly named excrement left by the crepe myrtle aphid. Sooty mold can be rubbed off your tree if it bothers you, but the best control begins with detection. Watch for ants (which feed on aphids), extra shiny leaves in spring and summer, and stunted, curled new growth. These are all indications of aphid activity. Spray infested trees with a stiff stream of water or insecticidal soap, doing your best to coat both sides of leaves. This will remove the aphids and, in turn, reduce the formation of sooty mold.

## FUNGAL LEAF SPOT

Wet, humid summers are conducive to fungal leaf spot in crepe myrtles. Spots appear first on lower leaves and then spread upward through the tree. Foliage may yellow and drop. Though most crepe myrtles survive, an infestation is both unsightly and unhealthy. Control with a fungicide that includes the name *Cercospora lythracearum,* the responsible fungus, on its label per manufacturer directions. If you live where summer rainfall is normally high, consider the following planting crepe myrtles that have been identified as resistant to fungal leaf spot as well as powdery mildew:

'APPALACHEE': light lavender
'CADDO': light pink
'FANTASY': white
'SIOUX': bright pink
'TONTO': red
'TUSKEGEE' and 'TUSCARORA': dark pink

## NAMED SELECTIONS

With their kaleidoscope of colors, numerous named selections of crepe myrtle are available. The National Arboretum bred crepe myrtles with improved resistance to powdery mildew and named them after Native American tribes. Here's a sample. For photos and more choices, go to: www.usna.usda.gov/PhotoGallery/CrapemyrtleGallery/CrapeTable.html.

'CHEROKEE': watermelon
'CHOCTAW': pink
'MIAMI': dark coral pink
'MUSKOGEE': lavender
'NATCHEZ': white
'POTOMAC': cool pink
'SEMINOLE': medium pink
'SIOUX': dark pink
'TUSCARORA': warm pink

A

B

C

D

E

(A) Because crepe myrtles grow quickly, there's no need to invest in large starter trees.

(B) Though autumn is the best time to plant most trees, you're better off buying crepe myrtles in summer when they're in bloom. Otherwise, you may end up with a color that's different than what you expected.

(C) Suckers are little sprouts that shoot up from the base of plants. Remove crepe myrtle suckers while they're young so you don't end up with a huge clump of trunks.

(E) If you want to remove seeds to prompt more blossoms on a crepe myrtle, cut stems that are no thicker than a pencil. There's no need to cut larger branches or trunks.

(F) Spent seedpods add winter interest and do not harm crepe myrtle trees. It's fine to leave them in place.

A

B

C

Crepe myrtles not only tolerate poor, dry soil, they actually bloom more profusely during dry summers. Their roots don't mind confined conditions, and roots won't buckle paving. This easy-growing characteristic makes these trees excellent for planting in courtyards, parking areas, and along sidewalks and driveways. However, crepe myrtles aren't the best trees for planting near swimming pools or patios, as blossom shed messily.

It is only natural that crepe myrtles are prized for their bold summer flowers. However, these small trees are also valuable in the landscape for making the great outdoors seem comfortably people-sized. Planting a crepe myrtle beside a bench is like opening an umbrella of foliage; it makes the bench seem anchored in place instead of plopped into the landscape. Another asset the crepe myrtle can claim is bark that peels as trees age to reveal sleek, smooth trunks. The strikingly attractive bark and upright form of crepe myrtle is especially noticeable in winter when leaves are down.

(A) Crepe myrtles have exfoliating bark. The older trees are, the more the bark peels. The result is a striking pattern that's pretty year-round. 'Natchez', the white-blooming selection shown here, is noted for its cinnamon-colored peeling bark.
(B) The winter beauty of crepe myrtles in their natural form is unsurpassed.
*Landscape architect Robert E. Marvin*
(C) If left uncut, crepe myrtles grow to just the right size for sheltering benches, patios, decks, and other gathering spots.

# Ginkgo

Gingkos require sunshine and time, and that's about it. These slow-growing trees thrive in full sun, grow in just about every kind of soil, and tolerate pollution, confined root space, heat, and cold. They're resistant to diseases and pests, don't require much water, and live a long, long time. Best of all, ginkgos have phenomenal autumn color. Every leaf on the tree will turn bright yellow pretty much at the same time. When leaves drop, they all go at once. Fallen leaves retain their color for about a week, spreading a carpet of gold across the ground.

So why don't we grow more ginkgos? Quite a few Southern cities and colleges are doing just that, but many homeowners continue to overlook this excellent tree. Perhaps the somewhat transient nature of our society has curbed the appetite for trees that take a long time to get big. However, the gingko's slow rate of growth shouldn't knock it out of landscape contention. Even young trees turn the trademark yellow each autumn, and the fan-shaped leaves are an attractive bright green in summer. Besides, there's something to be said about planting a tree that's likely to live for generations. Plant a ginkgo to commemorate a birth, a memory, a wedding, or to ensure your own individual legacy. If your neighborhood is starting a street tree program, get ginkgo on the list. The roots won't disturb paving, and car exhaust won't disturb the trees. Even a handful of young ginkgos growing streetside will give your street a distinctive claim each autumn. Imagine roads lined with these kings of color.

Newer selections of this old-fashioned tree have been bred to grow vertically, so named selections of ginkgos don't require the large amount of space to spread that the species tree does. (*Gingko biloba* can grow 90 feet

## GETTING ACQUAINTED

Deciduous tree (bare in winter)

Size depends upon selection; after decades of growth, most top 50 feet

Distinctive conical tree shape

Brilliant golden autumn color

Good legacy tree, as ginkgos live for hundreds of years

Slow rate of growth

Roots will not harm paving

Good for urban conditions

Tolerant of heat and cold

All-day sun to mostly sunny

Any soil except wet

Good choice for planting along streets, in parking areas, large patios, estates, and open lawns

Pairs well with lawns; shows off nicely with a background of Leyland cypress

Zones 4–9

*Trees: Showy*

Though they grow slowly, ginkgos get large and live for generations.

A

B

(A) Hold that rake. Gingko leaves retain their golden color for days after they fall to the ground.
(B) If I were in charge of naming paint colors, I'd name one gingko gold. The autumn foliage of this tree is legendary.

tall and over 45 feet in width.) The newer, upright selections have smaller spreads, but they still grow too tall to plant beneath overhead lines. If you avoid power lines, ginkgos are excellent for planting as street trees, along sidewalks, in parking areas, or in open lawns.

The gingko tree is a glimpse into the ancient past. The veins of each gingko leaf fan outward from the stem without crossing or touching, and the fruit exhibits a primitive form not found in other plants today. These ancient characteristics earn the gingko the nickname "living fossil." Real fossils many millions of years old reveal imprints of leaves virtually indistinguishable from the ginkgo you can grow in your landscape today. The unusual leaves are easy to identify, making them a must-have for school leaf collection projects. Children love to play with the leathery leaves, too, especially in autumn when the fallen foliage resembles thousands of little golden fans.

## BAD GIRLS AND GOOD BOYS

Ginkgos have separate female and male trees. Unfortunately, both sexes of the tree were for sale years ago, so both were planted. Female trees bear fruit with a strong odor that drops to the ground and has earned unflattering comparisons to dog doo. Needless to say, these stinkers have given a good tree a bad reputation. Today, you can buy male clone gingko trees that will never produce fruit. Read plant tags and buy a named selection to be assured of an odor-free tree.

'MAGYAR': pyramidal form; 50 feet high by 30 feet wide
'PRINCETON SENTRY': also sold as PNI 2720; narrow form; 40 feet high by 15 feet wide
'AUTUMN GOLD' and 'LAKEVIEW': both selections are reliably male, but studies have shown that they may no longer be genetically true and may result in crooked trunks

# Kousa Dogwood

T hough you may consider dogwoods to be exclusively shade-loving trees, here's one that likes the sun: the kousa dogwood. This species of dogwood thrives in full sun and blooms later than the dogwoods you see growing in the woods. Kousa blossoms don't appear until after leaves have appeared, so these trees can't claim that dainty blossoms-floating-in-air look that's characteristic of wild dogwoods, *Cornus florida*. Kousa flowers wait until mid to late spring to open, a good three weeks to a month after native dogwoods have bloomed. But when kousas do get around to blooming, they go all out—the trees are covered. The combination of green foliage and white flowers is stunning, and the show lasts for weeks.

Kousa dogwoods are resistant to anthracnose, a problem that has plagued native dogwood populations. Kousas are also more drought tolerant. Virtually indistinguishable from a variety called Chinese dogwood, the carefree kousa dogwood is often touted as a solution to the decline of wild dogwoods. But this tree isn't for planting in the woods; you'll need to choose an open spot with plenty of sun and room for your kousa to grow. Young kousa dogwoods are upright and shaped somewhat like umbrellas, but canopies become more irregular as plants mature. Trees eventually reach 20 to 30 feet high, with a spread nearly as wide. The branches of mature trees dip gracefully to the ground and should not be removed, so plan ahead and plant your kousa away from places where people need to walk or drive. One charming feature of this tree is the way branches assume the appearance of horizontal lay-

ers, adding a note of elegance to the arrangement of flowers and foliage. (Technically, the flower is the green ball in the center and what look like petals are actually colored leaves called bracts, much like the red "petals" on a poinsettia.) Leaves turn shades of scarlet in autumn before dropping for the winter.

*Cornus kousa*

Also sold Chinese dogwood, *Cornus kousa* 'Chinensis', *Cornus kousa* var. *chinensis*

### GETTING ACQUAINTED

Deciduous tree (bare in winter)

20 to 30 feet high by 15 to 25 feet wide

Large, white flowers appear after leaves in mid to late spring

Slow rate of growth

Resistant to anthracnose

Full sun to partial shade

Acidic, well-drained soil rich in organic matter; will tolerate somewhat alkaline, poor soil

Good choice for anchoring a sunny bed, standing alone as a lawn specimen, or filling a corner of the landscape; attractive when spilling over a low picket fence

Pairs well with Anthony Waterer spirea, Flower Carpet® rose, or liriope

Zones 4–8

*Trees: Showy*

Kousa dogwood flowers appear after foliage, making a striking green-and-white combination that continues for weeks.

A

B

C

(A) Like the flowers of native dogwoods, kousa dogwood blooms are large, white, flat, and four-petaled, but kousa petals are pointy, not rounded like those of wild dogwoods.

(B) Fruit of the kousa dogwood starts off green and turns red in late summer, resembling little pebbled cherries.

(C) Kousa dogwoods are not highly tolerant of drought or urban conditions, but they are tougher than the native dogwoods that flower on bare branches in early spring. Profuse kousa flowers are arranged in rows with foliage.

## AGING GRACEFULLY

A kousa dogwood that stands alone gives ample opportunity to admire this graceful tree from all sides. When planting a kousa dogwood in a lawn, be prepared to sacrifice a circle of grass in the future. As the tree grows older and larger, branches will dip nearly to ground level, casting deep shade beneath a low canopy. Don't chop off the bottom branches to try to reclaim this insignificant amount of grass. Simply widen the mulch bed as the tree matures.

Kousa dogwoods prefer acidic, well-drained soil. They'll tolerate slightly alkaline soil but don't try to grow them in areas with very high soil pH. (Homeowners with such soil should substitute the lilac chaste-tree.) When planting a kousa dogwood in clay soil, mix one part sand and one part chunky compost or pine bark with one part native soil. Position the root-ball so it sits a few inches above the level of existing clay; mound new soil as needed to keep the rootball covered. In any soil, mulch around kousa trunks—but not against them—to discourage weed growth. You'll have to pull any weeds that sneak through the mulch. All dogwoods have delicate bark, so damage from string trimmers and mowers can be deadly to these beautiful trees.

# Kwanzan Cherry

*Prunus serrulata* 'Kwanzan'

Also sold as 'Interstem', Kwanzan Japanese flowering cherry, sekiyama, hisakura

You'll buy Kwanzan cherry for its luscious pink ruffled spring flowers, but you'll enjoy it year-round. This little tree is a true four-season beauty. The short trunk, branches angling up like arms held aloft, and dense spreading canopy make the Kwanzan cherry attractive whether it is in bloom, green with leaves, sporting autumn colors, or even completely bare.

Flowers arrive in midspring, which is later than other flowering cherries, and the blooms last longer, too. Dangling, dark pink buds make an appearance just as new, bronze-tinted leaves begin unfurling. The buds open nearly all at once to line each branch with drooping pom-poms of pink. The generously sized, cotton-candy-colored flowers are double, which means they're so packed with petals they become clusters of fluff.

Petals drop as leaves mature, and by late spring the entire tree is an umbrella of green. Kwanzan cherries cast nice little circles of shade in summer, but sunlight slanting beneath the crown means you can grow grass beneath them. Just take care to surround trees with thick beds of mulch that don't touch the trunks, and avoid using string trimmers or mowers near them. The bark is thin and delicate, and wounds can become entry points for disease.

As pretty as they are in spring and as lush as they are in summer, Kwanzan cherries earn their keep in autumn, too. Leaves turn shades of yellow and bronze before dropping like a puddle of color on the ground. The smooth, shiny gray bark, marked with orange dashed-line rings, shows up well in winter when branches are bare. Kwanzan cherries rarely require pruning, so let their natural shape

## GETTING ACQUAINTED

Deciduous tree (bare in winter)

Often 12 to 20 feet high by 10 to 15 feet wide, but size depends on rootstock; when grown on its own stock, may grow 30 to 40 feet high by 20 to 25 feet wide

Very showy pink spring flowers cover trees in spring; foliage is colorful in autumn

Rapid rate of growth

Full sun

Moist, well-drained soil

Not for urban conditions

Good choice for open lawn areas or in the vicinity of entryways and patios; do not plant, pave, mow, or trim close to the trunk

Pairs well with lawns, liriope, and Flower Carpet® roses

Zones 6–8

*When grown in the correct soil—moist, well drained, and reasonably fertile—Kwanzan cherries don't need much supplemental fertilizer.*

**AUTUMN**

**SUMMER**

**WINTER**

**SPRING**

## BUYING HEALTHY TREES

Kwanzan cherries were once so prone to viral problems that many landscape architects stopped recommending them for a while. But a government-led effort to develop viral-free stock has improved the outlook for many flowering fruit trees, both ornamental and edible. It is critical that you look for the initials VC on the plant tag before purchasing a Kwanzan cherry, as this indicates that you're buying a "virus-certified" tree. If possible, purchase directly from a grower and ask if virus-indexed bud wood has been used on virus-certified rootstock. If the answer is yes, you're likely to enjoy a healthy tree for a good twenty years or more. Baby cherry trees inoculated with NOGALL® also resist crown gall, another problem common in cherries. The long and short of it is, Kwanzan cherries are wonderful trees that can grow in your garden carefree if you start off with a healthy, disease-resistant plant and give it the right conditions. So get your crepe myrtles from a discount garden center, but order or purchase your Kwanzan cherries from a reliable grower who won't hesitate to share virus fighting strategies with customers.

TREES: SHOWY

A

B

C

reign. Selectively prune only as needed to remove any branches that are dead or that are rubbing across other branches.

Keep in mind that Kwanzan cherries prefer well-drained soil and will decline in situations where the soil is compacted or holds water. Mix equal parts rich compost and sand with native soil at planting. When grown in the correct soil, Kwanzan cherries don't need much supplemental fertilizer. If you do feed trees, make sure the nitrogen is slow-release and apply it in early spring before blooms. Avoid fertilizing in autumn, as this may promote new growth that can be damaged by coming cold snaps. Trees grown in lawns may receive excessive nitrogen and probably should not be fertilized. Though they dislike water puddling around roots, these trees do like regular water during hot summers, so they're great for landscapes that have sprinkler systems as long as the site drains well. Established trees tolerate dry spells better than young ones, but Kwanzan cherries should not be considered drought resistant. Gardeners in frost-free areas should substitute redbud.

The small size of this tree makes it ideal for growing beside a walkway, before a blank wall, or next to a patio. Plant trees in lawns or sunny beds of low groundcover. You can grow a single Kwanzan cherry as a specimen tree, or plant a double row of them to create a formal tunnel effect known as an *allée*. This tree is easy to grow in matched pairs but should only be planted this way in a landscape that is fairly symmetrical to start with. Pairs will look odd in an informal landscape; use odd-numbers of one, three, or five trees instead. Grow in full sun.

*Trees: Showy*

(A) Rose-pink buds dangle beneath the emerging leaves of Kwanzan cherry in early spring.
(B) The puffy pink flowers of Kwanzan cherry sit like fat wreathes on stems.
(C) Distinctive orange ridges marking shiny gray bark are noticeable when leaves drop.

KWANZAN CHERRY

97

# Lilac Chaste-tree

*Vitex agnus-castus*

Also sold as vitex, chaste-tree,
monk's pepper, chastetree,
summer lilac
Not to be confused with another
plant called chastetree (*Vitex negundo*),
which survives colder winters but
doesn't flower as heavily

## GETTING ACQUAINTED

Deciduous tree (bare in winter)

15 to 20 high by 8 to 12 feet wide

Showy, fragrant, violet-blue blossoms attract
butterflies and hummingbirds in summer

Rapid rate of growth

May produce unwanted seedlings in frost-free
areas

Tolerant of urban conditions

Full sun to mostly sunny; thrives in heat

Any soil except wet

Good choice for open areas, hillsides, low-
water landscapes, sidewalk planting,
screening

Pairs well with lawns, sundrops primrose, liriope, garlic chives, butterfly bush, Mexican
bush sage, and glossy abelia

Zones 7–9

In the right conditions, lilac chaste-trees can
be long-lived. Older plants may be left uncut
or selectively pruned to form a small tree by
exposing the trunks.

When spring fever hits and you find yourself at a nursery, take a second look at that stick in a pot that other shoppers are passing by. Lilac chase-tree is notoriously slow to sprout leaves in spring, but have faith that beauty is on the way. When these small trees flower in summer, they're stunning. Aromatic violet to lavender flowers appear in early to midsummer as spikes of color held above the leaves. Butterflies, hummingbirds, and bees find lilac chaste-tree flowers highly attractive. (Some people call these plants "butterfly bushes," though they're not to be confused with *Buddleia davidii*.)

After a big show in early to midsummer, lilac chaste-tree blooms sporadically into autumn. Despite a somewhat shrubby shape, a lilac chaste-tree can to grow 15 to 20 high in a hot climate, making it a small tree in the Southern landscape. Most chaste-trees have multiple stems and grow as large clumps. A little pruning on the undersides is needed to encourage a more treelike shape. Or, keep the clump and enjoy chaste-trees as a thick background plant. They're valuable for hard-to-fill hot spots and areas beyond reach of a hose.

All-day sun produces the most flowers. Mostly sunny areas will do, but a half-day's sun is just barely enough. Chaste-trees grown in deep shade will fare poorly and rarely flower. Lilac chaste-tree, also called vitex, is an attractive choice for planting beside patios, parking areas, sidewalks, and in butterfly gardens. It thrives on neglect and can grow on sunny slopes and roadsides. You can grow a lilac chaste-tree beside a swimming pool deck if you don't mind bees that busily crawl over the flowers. Set chaste-trees about 6 feet behind beds. This gives these dense plants room to grow and keeps you from digging too much around their roots, which don't

A

B

C

D

(A) Shades of blue and lavender are always welcome in hot landscapes. You can cut off the faded blooms of lilac chaste-trees in summer before they set seed to prompt a second crop of flowers in autumn.

(B) Lilac chaste-trees are in no way related to lilacs that grow in northern states; lilac merely refers to the color of the blooms.

(C) It's not what you're thinking. It's lilac chase-tree foliage.

(D) Freeze-damaged lilac chaste-trees can be cut back to nearly ground level to encourage fresh growth. Multiple new canes usually produce large, clumping plants. There's no need to cut down healthy plants, but you can shape them in late winter.

care to be disturbed. Lilac chaste-tree rarely becomes tall enough to conflict with overhead lines.

Lilac chaste-trees will grow in any kind of soil except permanently wet. The high pH of alkaline soil is no problem, nor is the low pH of acidic soil. Lilac chaste-trees thrive in poor, dry soil and bright, hot sun. Even high humidity is no foe for this tough little tree. Avoid overwatering. It is especially important to refrain from watering trees in autumn, so they can toughen up for winter. Lilac chaste-trees produce gray-green, palmately compound foliage with five to seven radiating leaflets, which is a horticultural way of saying the leaves resemble marijuana. So if your neighbors start looking at you funny, show them this book.

LILAC CHASTE-TREE

**NAMED SELECTIONS**

'ABBEVILLE BLUE': rich blue flower spikes 12 to 18 inches long

'ALBA': white flowers

'COLONIAL BLUE': medium blue flowers; adapts to training as a single-trunked tree

'LILAC QUEEN': lavender flowers have a pink tint; trees regularly reach 20 feet in height

'MISSISSIPPI BLUE': lavender-blue flowers; heavy bloomer

'MONTROSE PURPLE': deep purple flowers; plants rarely grow taller than 8 to 10 feet

'ROSEA': pink flowers

*Magnolia* x *soulangiana*

Also sold as Oriental magnolia, Japanese magnolia, Chinese magnolia

## GETTING ACQUAINTED

Deciduous tree (bare in winter)

20 to 30 feet high and wide; usually has multiple trunks

Very showy pink-to-white flowers in spring

Moderate rate of growth

Full sun

Any well-drained soil

Good choice for use as stand-alone lawn tree or grown as an accent beside entryways, patios, and decks

Pairs well with lawns, Siberian iris, bridalwreath spirea, liriope, and spring-blooming bulbs

Zones 5–9

Saucer magnolias spread wide canopies given the opportunity, but they'll adapt to fit available space as they grow.

# Saucer Magnolia

When saucer magnolias are in bloom, everyone who doesn't have one wants one. This tree's large flowers start off as big fuzzy buds that last through winter. By early spring, the buds have become candles of color—tightly wrapped columns of pink or purple that stand up straight. Then, a warm spell or a bit of sunshine convinces the tree to unfurl its flowers and each candle opens to a large, saucer-shaped blossom. Opened flowers are lighter in color than the candles, appearing shell pink, white, or something in between. Trees are covered with blossoms. The fact that blooms appear well before leaves makes the show even more spectacular.

But spring is a fickle season, and warm spells can be fleeting. It's not uncommon for a blast of winter to suddenly show up and spoil the show. Saucer magnolia flowers zapped by cold can turn from pink to brown overnight. (If your tree is in bloom and temperatures are set to drop dramatically, snip a branch tip with blossoms attached and bring it inside to enjoy the color and fragrance a little longer.) Though distressing to homeowners, the ruined blossoms do not adversely affect the health of the plant. The saucer magnolia is an optimistic tree; cold-damaged flowers one year do nothing to deter blooming the following spring. And whenever spring does manage to bring a full flower show, you'll know it was worth the wait.

One way to increase the odds of successful flowering is to avoid planting saucer magnolias in a southern exposure. Even a slight delay in bloom time can make a big difference in preventing cold damage. Trees planted away from those early rays of southern sun wait a little longer to open blooms, sometimes dodging late cold snaps. Saucer magnolias require a lot

The lightly fragrant blossoms of saucer magnolia appear before the leaves.

of sun to flower well, so plant yours where it will receive as much as possible while avoiding a southern exposure. A little shade is fine, especially if it's from trees that lose their leaves in winter. However, dense shade can make your saucer magnolia lean crookedly toward sunlight and flower sparsely. Saucer magnolias can take the heat, so there's no reason to avoid hot, western sun, even in summer. All-day sun is fine.

This tree isn't picky about soil, though good drainage is a good idea. Slightly acidic soil (low soil pH) is a plus, but saucer magnolias are highly adaptable, so homeowners in areas of alkaline soil can plant them, too. Another appealing feature of the saucer magnolia is its ability to bloom when the tree is quite young. It is always nice to be rewarded for your planting efforts without having to wait years and years, especially as this

SAUCER MAGNOLIA

### OFF-SEASON FLOWERS

Plants that bloom out of season can be a little alarming. Rest assured that it is perfectly normal for the saucer magnolia to blossom sporadically in summer and even during hot autumn days. Such flowering doesn't indicate anything is wrong with the tree, and next spring's show won't be reduced.

A

B

C

(A) Planting a saucer magnolia brings spring to
your garden early.
(B) Saucer magnolia blooms when quite young,
so you don't have to wait for many years to enjoy
springtime flowers.
(C) Summer foliage is dense enough to provide a
circle of shade.

tree isn't easy to transplant when larger. A single saucer magnolia standing alone in a lawn is truly a sight to behold in spring. Though the leaves that show up later are large, the summer canopy of this tree is somewhat open, allowing some sunlight to reach grass grown beneath it. Saucer magnolias that have been selectively pruned in their youth to create a more upright form allow more sun beneath their canopies than low-branched, unpruned trees. Because the crown is naturally very low for many years, there's not much room to walk beneath one that's never been pruned. Start early to train the ones you plant near sidewalks or patios.

To shape a saucer magnolia, remove only the lowest branches and do so when the tree is young. Most saucer magnolias have multiple trunks. There's no need to remove trunks to make your tree a single-trunked standard unless space dictates you do so or you simply like the look. Keep in mind that pruning must be done early in a tree's life. Chopping off big branches later on makes trees awkward in appearance. It may also cause trunk wounds that never heal. Though saucer magnolias are durable, oozing trunk wounds can adversely affect the tree's health.

Saucer magnolias left alone to grow in their natural form make lovely trees. The low branches and multiple trunks give the tree dramatic presence. The generous spread of branches produces large crops of spring flowers. Give unpruned saucer magnolias plenty of room to grow—these trees can easily grow 20 to 30 feet wide and tall. Saucer magnolias assume a rather mounded shape until maturity, by which time they've formed higher, more irregularly shaped canopies.

When the saucer magnolia is not in bloom, it is a good citizen in the landscape but makes no other attempt to call attention to itself. Summer foliage is a medium green. Autumn color, such that it is, rates a dull yellow. Leaf drop requires raking. Winter is actually an attractive time for this tree as its open form, bare branches, fuzzy buds, and smooth gray bark have understated appeal.

# Trees for Privacy

# Leyland Cypress

x *Cupressocyparis leylandii*

H ere's a fast-growing tree that lets you put privacy where you need it. The Leyland cypress stays dense and dark green year-round, making it the perfect choice for keeping passersby from looking into your garden or home. This tree is also valuable for blocking views you don't want to see, such as your neighbor's garage or dog pen.

This evergreen's distinctive shape is narrow and pyramidal. Although Leyland cypresses broaden with age, they'll always remain taller than they are wide. Even in maturity, thick foliage adheres to the original compact

form. Though they can easily reach 70 feet in height, most Leyland cypress rarely grow more than 15 to 20 feet wide, so you can squeeze a row of them in along a narrow stretch of property. The tight foliage also takes shearing well—if you want to make the effort, you can confine a tree's spread even more to keep it suitable for a restricted space. But it won't be long before your Leyland cypress is taller than you can reach.

The fact that Leylands grow tall but remain dense makes them ideal for solving privacy problems posed by multiple-story houses adjacent to your property. The trees' narrow shapes are also good for screening public sidewalks or streets close

to your home. The trunk of each tree is nearly completely hidden by branches and foliage, so any views beyond a Leyland cypress are blocked from the ground up. The solid dark green shape is excellent in the background of a garden. Bright plants show off better when there's something dark behind them and when other views aren't distracting. The evergreen presence of Leyland cypress helps mask the winter absence of perennials and improves the sight of cold, bare branches.

Perhaps best of all, you won't have to wait forever for your living screen to do its job. Leyland cypress gets big fast, growing as much as

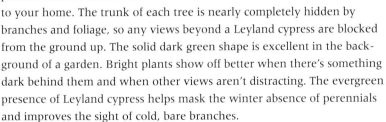

**GETTING ACQUAINTED**

Evergreen tree

50 to 80 feet high by 15 to 20 feet wide

Uniformly shaped, makes a solid green wall in the landscape; trees branched nearly to the ground

Rapid rate of growth

All-day sun to mostly sunny

Any soil that's well drained; not for wet soil

Good choice for blocking undesirable views, adding privacy, establishing a background in the landscape; narrow form makes it useful for growing along property lines, between houses, beside parking areas and tall buildings

Provides a good background for burning bush, Anthony Waterer spirea, bridalwreath spirea, butterfly bush, Flower Carpet® rose, and Mexican bush sage; mixes well with white pine and river birch for screening

Zones 6–9

Because Leyland cypresses remain unchanged, these evergreen trees highlight the seasonal attributes of other plants.

Trees: Privacy

## DRAWBACKS

### BAGWORMS

Unfortunately, Leyland cypress foliage is a favorite food of bagworms. If you notice gray or brown woody pods on your tree, pick them off or spray right away. Each bag containers a hungry caterpillar. If you wait, a mild infestation can spread, damaging or killing several trees in a row. Spray with a pesticide labeled bagworm killer, taking care to follow manufacturer's recommendations for application rates and safety measures. Repeat applications may be necessary if more defoliation is noticeable. If you don't like to use pesticides, removing all the bags by hand and destroying them is necessary. Do not allow bags to remain on trees through the winter, as new eggs may hatch.

It's important to mix other kinds of trees with Leyland cypress when space permits. That will help stop the spread of problems, such as bagworms, which have killed this tree and threaten the entire row.

One way to discourage bagworm infestations is to interplant Leyland cypress with other kinds of trees and encourage neighbors to do the same. Neighborhoods that depend heavily on Leyland cypresses in the landscape may be more susceptible to an eventual decline in the trees' health—growing a lot of the same kind of plant is always risky. Known as a monoculture, this planting practice establishes potential hosts in quantity for diseases or pests that prefer a single species. Growing Leylands together in a row makes it easier for pests to spread. In addition, the loss of a single tree, for whatever reason, is less noticeable when several different kinds of trees are grown together.

### CANKER

Leyland cypresses are also susceptible to *Seiridium* canker, a fatal disease characterized by browning branches and oozing sap. Though the only solution is to remove and replace any infected trees, you can minimize the chances of Leyland cypress getting this problem by keeping trunks free of wounds. Always mulch heavily beneath these trees, so you won't need to use mowers or string trimmers near trunks. Many injury-free Leyland cypresses never have any problems.

### FROST-FREE SUBSTITUTE

Coastal climates and other areas with extremely hot summer temperatures, high humidity, and lots of summer rain are not the best places to grow Leyland cypress. Grow southern red cedar (*Juniperus silicicola*) instead. This evergreen tree is a tough, heat-tolerant cousin of the eastern red cedar (*Juniperus virginiana*). If you can't find the southern species, the eastern red cedar will do nicely.

### BUDGET MINDED

Plant privacy trees in a zigzag formation for a screen that becomes effective more quickly. The staggered layout is almost like having a double row of trees, though you'll only need to buy a few more trees than you would for a single row.

1 to 3 feet taller each year. For fastest growth, plant trees in rich, moist but well-drained soil. Trees planted in poor soil will thrive but will grow at the slower rate. Plant in full sun and avoid soil that stays damp. It doesn't matter whether soil is acidic or alkaline: Leyland cypress isn't picky as long as its roots are not wet.

A

B

C

(A) Fast growth, evergreen foliage, and an upright form has made Leyland cypress a favorite tree for adding privacy.
(B) The needle-shaped foliage of Leyland cypresses has a feathery texture.
(C) Leyland cypresses make a dense, evergreen background for deciduous trees and shrubs.

# River Birch

*Betula nigra*

Also sold as Heritage® birch, Dura-Heat® birch

This tree grows up fast. If watered regularly, a river birch can easily increase 3 feet or more in height each year with proportional canopy growth. Blazing full sun is fine, and there's no reason to avoid planting river birch in hot afternoon sun. In fact, these rapid growth trees are good choices for providing shade in spots that are just too hot to enjoy otherwise. You'll enjoy winter rays after leaves are down, so go ahead and position river birch where it can cast shade to cool too-hot rooms in your house, too.

Native to the Southeast, river birches grow naturally in moist areas and, as you'd guess, along riverbanks. But what this tree's name doesn't tell you is that the river birch can also adapt to drier soil and will even grow in parking and patio areas, where heat reflected from paving would distress lesser trees. River birch roots won't buckle paving, either. Supplemental watering is required for all new river birches during their first hot season, but trees learn to toughen up after that. Unless your goal is to promote the most growth in the shortest amount of time, you'll only have to water established trees during true drought conditions. Even river birches left to their own devices grow fast enough to noticeably increase in size each year. River birches prefer neutral to acidic soil but will adapt to high soil pH levels, too. Trees grown in extremely alkaline soil may require supplemental iron every once in a while if foliage turns yellowish during spring or summer.

Many kinds of beautiful birches cannot survive our hot, humid climate—when planted in the South, they decline and die. But river birches are native to our region, so they can take the heat. This makes them less susceptible to borers and other problems that plague cold-loving birches

## GETTING ACQUAINTED

Deciduous tree (bare in winter)

40 to 70 feet high by 40 to 50 feet wide

Peeling cream-and-tan bark is attractive; trees usually have multiple trunks

Rapid rate of growth

Thrives in urban conditions but may require supplemental water

Heat tolerant

Full sun to partial sun

When established, will tolerate any kind of soil, from wet to dry

Good choice for filtering views and adding privacy, planting near decks, patios, parking areas, and driveways

Pairs well with Leyland cypress and white pine to form screens; also pairs well with liriope, nandina, glossy abelia

Zones 4–9

Both practical and pretty, river birches don't mind heat and thrive in soil that's wet or dry, and their roots won't crack paving.

A

B

C

(A) River birches thrive in full sun. They'll also grow in shade, though shade-grown trees will bend toward the sun.

(B) River birches grow quickly. Planting these trees in the landscapes of new homes will help get rid of that bulldozed-lot look.

(C) River birches develop their characteristic peeling bark young, so you won't have to wait for years to enjoy it.

## PRUNING

River birches don't require much upkeep. Trees usually have multiple trunks. To maintain a cluster of five to seven main trunks, occasionally remove suckers that sprout from the base of trunks to prevent them from developing into additional trunks. Don't prune limbs unless you must make room to walk or drive beneath them. Make such cuts in autumn to avoid oozing spring sap.

## APHID ATTACKS

Young river birches are susceptible to aphids when tender leaves first unfurl in spring. If foliage appears shiny and stunted or attracts ants, aphids are the likely culprits. It is unlikely that the pests will do permanent damage to the tree. For particularly bad infestations, spray foliage with a systemic pesticide that includes both aphids and birches on the label. Follow manufacturer's directions. For organic treatment, spray with a stiff stream of water or insecticidal soap. Dura-Heat® river birches are reputed to be aphid resistant.

## MULTI-TRUNKED TREES

You can buy river birches as standards (trees with single trunks) or as multiple-trunked trees. Unless your space is limited, trees with multiple trunks are the best choice. This form lends more presence to the landscape and is the most effective for screening. More trunks mean more peeling bark to enjoy, too.

that become stressed by high temperatures. Two cultivated river birch selections, Heritage® and Dura-Heat®, are particularly noted for their abilities to withstand heat, leafspot, and bronze birch borers.

In addition to its quick growth and adaptability, the river birch is known for attractive peeling bark that curls from trunks in papery layers. The older trees get, the more dramatic their bark becomes. Creamy layers expose cinnamon-colored undercoats. The Heritage river birch also includes a salmon tint in the color palette of its bark. The rough, peeling bark of all river birches boasts a coarse texture, making these trees a good match for landscapes that include stone in paving, walls, or foundations. Although trunks are pretty year-round, they become especially noticeable after leaves drop in autumn and slender branches are bare. The scarcity of color in the winter landscape makes river birch bark more conspicuous, qualifying this tree as valuable all year.

Because river birches are among the fastest growing of Southern trees, they're very useful for filtering views. Though they won't block sights completely, these trees can form good-looking buffers that enhance privacy. Plant a grove of river birches to downplay a busy street, screen a poor view, or create a degree of separation among areas within your landscape. River birches make lovely background plants and can form living partitions along property lines, but plant these informally shaped trees in groups, not straight rows. Branches that dip gracefully downward increase the river birch's ability to screen views and add privacy. Dura-Heat river birches are known to have denser canopies than the species plants, another asset of this heat-loving selection.

A single river birch is useful as a specimen tree. This means you can set just one tree where it will command attention. Entry areas, patios, front gardens, side yards, courtyards, and rear landscapes are all excellent spots for adding a river birch. Consider views from inside your home looking outward, too. A river birch can add interest to a dull corner or blank wall. Or, plant one beside a deck to add greenery up high while providing summer shade and privacy. Just make sure you give your tree plenty of room to spread its wide canopy and be prepared to clean up messy leaves. Some homeowners prefer to keep river birches away from rooftops because the leaf drop is quite heavy in autumn. But others consider leaves on the roof a worthwhile tradeoff for a pretty tree that grows fast enough to make a brand new house quickly look at home on its site. Tall houses are particularly well complemented by river birches because these trees quickly reach heights that are proportionate to upper stories. For best results, plant river birch 15 feet or more away from foundations.

Peeling, papery bark is an attractive feature of the river birch year-round.

*Trees: Privacy*

*Pinus strobus*

Also sold as eastern white pine, soft pine, northern pine, northern white pine

**GETTING ACQUAINTED**

Evergreen tree

50 to 100 feet high by 25 to 40 feet wide

Full-to-the-ground Christmas tree shape; fluffy bluish green needles are present all year

Rapid rate of growth

Not tolerant of urban conditions

Thrives in areas with cold winter temperatures, mild but humid summers

Easy to transplant

Full sun to dappled shade

Any soil but alkaline

Good choice for adding privacy, blocking views, providing a background

Pairs well with river birch, Leyland cypress; good background for deciduous shrubs

Zone 3 to upper zone 8

Branches grow from the trunk in levels, creating perfect symmetry.

# White Pine

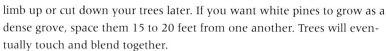

Here's a great tree to plant when you want a living wall of year-round greenery. Just make sure you allow plenty of room for white pine to grow. Given the right conditions, these trees grow rapidly; yours may top 50 feet before you pay off the mortgage. But as long as white pines aren't located under power lines, it isn't the height that's generally the problem—it is the spread. White pines are conical trees, with low branches that skirt the central trunk in a widening circle that may eventually reach 40 feet across.

Far too often, this elegant tree is planted where it will out-grow its space, so homeowners resort to chopping off branches from the lower 10 feet of the tree. The result is sadly comical, like a half-shaved Persian cat. Avoid this landscape faux pas by planting white pines well away from routes where people must walk or drive. Setting young white pines a good 25 feet back from sidewalks, patios, decks, and driveways will save you the agony of deciding whether to limb up or cut down your trees later. If you want white pines to grow as a dense grove, space them 15 to 20 feet from one another. Trees will eventually touch and blend together.

The beauty of the white pine is in its form and its long, fluffy needles. Each tree features a very straight single trunk that grows very tall. Branches arranged in perfect circles around the trunk grow straight out from it, as if someone drilled holes in rings around a telephone pole and inserted fake branches. Young white pines are Christmas-tree shaped, but trees grow more round-topped with age and branches curl upward a little at the ends. The long, bluish green needles seem to shimmer in a sunny breeze; if you look closely, you can see a thin white line on each needle. White pines hold onto their needles for two years, then shed them discreetly as new ones take their place. Bottom branches close to

B

ground level help hide fallen needles. Healthy white pines are never brown or bare.

White pines are easy to grow if they like their environment. To keep trees content, avoid planting in alkaline soil (areas with lots of limestone but no azaleas). Acidic soils are preferable. A wide range of soils will do, from moist and rich to thin and rocky. Clay, sand, well drained, or poorly drained—all these soil types are agreeable as long as the white pine gets a good taste of winter each year. With a shorter taproot than most pines, young white pines are easy to transplant.

Plant white pines in full sun for fast-growing, uniformly shaped trees. Native to many parts of the eastern United States, white pines grow wild in the woods where sunlight is reduced. However, such shaded trees are generally slower growing and may become spindly. White pines are fond of winter. Gardeners in frost-free and rare-frost areas ought to grow red cedar instead (see page 106).

White pines are extremely valuable for adding privacy and blocking unwanted views. Homeowners would do well to include white pines in the mix—provided they've got the space—when planting rows of Leyland cypress as a screen. Doing so ensures that something evergreen will still be standing if bagworms wipe out the Leyland cypress. The contrast between dark green Leyland cypress and bluish green white pines makes for an attractive color combination year-round, another reason to pair these trees together.

**(A)** White pines make a dense, fluffy screen that stays green year-round. Plant them where you don't need to walk or drive beneath the branches. These trees are best left unpruned with a full skirt of branches that reach the ground.
**(B)** White stripes on long needles give this tree its name.

WHITE PINE

**SEPARATE THESE TWO**
Don't plant white pine within a quarter mile of gooseberry or currant bushes, which serve as the alternate host for white pine blister rust, a serious fungal threat to these trees.

# Trees for Shade

# Drake Elm

*Ulmus parvifolia* 'Drake'

Also sold as lacebark elm, Chinese elm
Not to be confused with Siberian elm
(*Ulmus pumila*), a large tree susceptible
to beetle damage

The Drake elm has more important things to do than bloom. So if it is color you're after, plant a crepe myrtle. But if you're seeking a tough little tree that grows fast and casts pleasing shade, read on. Drake elms tolerate heat, drought, and urban conditions such as pollution, reflected heat from paving, and restricted root space. This makes them ideal for planting along roadsides, driveways, sidewalks, and near parking areas. The bark peels as trees age, giving trunks interesting gray and orange patterns. With small leaves and downward swaying branch tips, a Drake elm is a graceful addition to the landscape—but one that's plain enough to avoid competing for attention with more colorful, showier plants.

The Drake elm is a lollipop tree, usually found for sale with a single trunk topped by a graceful rounded canopy of drooping branches. Their small size—a maximum of about 40 feet high and wide—and low canopy means these trees are good for making outdoor spaces feel comfortably people-sized. You can plant Drake elms beside patios, in courtyards, or at entryways. This tree grows quickly, so you won't have long to wait for some additional shade.

The farther south you live, the greener your Drake elm will stay in winter. Trees in zone 7 tend to lose most but not quite all of their leaves during the cold months, while Drake elms growing in zone 9 keep nearly the same appearance year-round.

## GETTING ACQUAINTED

Semi-evergreen tree

35 to 40 feet high by 35 to 40 feet wide

Tidy, round-headed tree; interesting bark

Rapid growth rate; provides quick shade

Tolerates drought, heat, pollution, and poor soil

Good for urban conditions

Resistant to insects and disease

All-day sun to partial shade

Any soil except wet

Good choice for planting near patios, parking areas, sidewalks, in lawns, and along streets

Pairs well with lawns, liriope, and Siberian iris

Zones 7–9

Trees: Shade

Drake elms prove that green need not be boring.

(A) Drake elms don't grow from seed. They're special trees propagated from cuttings, so read plant tags carefully to double check the name.

(B) The foliage of Drake elm turns yellow and drops in cold winters, but many leaves remain green and on the tree in areas with mild winters.

## SUPPORT SYSTEM

Newly planted Drake elms are top-heavy, with big crowns and thin trunks. It's necessary to support them with guy wires to keep transplants from twisting sideways or flopping over. After a complete growing season, fresh roots should hold the tree in place and you can remove the guy wires.

Though this tree is a zelkova, not a Drake elm, the principal of guying remains the same.

Run wires through cut sections of hose so wires won't cut into the tree. Loop each of three wires around a sturdy branch near the trunk. Anchor each wire to a stake in the ground. The three stakes should be spaced approximately 120 degrees apart at three points in a circle around the tree. Twist wire to make it taut. You may need to tighten the wire from time to time. It's a good idea to tie a big strip of brightly colored flagging tape to the center of each guy wire to make it clearly visible to pedestrians.

## BLIGHT FIGHTER

If there's an Elm Street in your town, chances are it was named for the once ubiquitous American elm (*Ulmus americana*). Entire populations of this large, stately shade tree have been wiped out since the arrival of Dutch elm disease on American soil in 1930. The smaller Drake elm is a named selection of Chinese elm (*Ulmus parvifolia*) that is resistant to this killer fungal infection.

## IT'S SUPPOSED TO DO THAT

Don't be alarmed when your Drake elm starts shedding bark. The attractive peeling bark is characteristic of this tree and gives rise to another name, lacebark elm. However, the thin delicate bark doesn't provide much protection, so take care to avoid damaging your Drake elm's trunk with mowers or string trimmers. Mulching a modest circle around trunks can help reduce the need for such equipment, but don't pile mulch like a termite mound surrounding the trunk.

# Red Maple

Red maples will thrive just about anywhere. They're known for growing in wet soil, which is why some people call them swamp maples. Surprisingly, red maples grow just as well in hot, confined planting areas. You'll find these trees thriving in parking lots and along city streets. Such adaptability gives you the choice of planting red maples in a range of settings from woodsy lots to formal gardens and even in parking areas that feature plenty of paving. Red maples with single trunks are more formal in appearance (and more commonly for sale) than trees with multiple trunks, so select ones that fill your need. You can also plant red maples within flood zones, beside ditches, ponds, lakes, and drainage areas. They are good choices for growing on the southern or southeastern side of your home or patio. The trees' leafy canopies will provide cooling shade in summer. When leaves are down, warming winter rays filter through the bare branches.

Besides being incredibly easy to grow, red maples earn their keep with an attractive color scheme that changes with the seasons. Bare branches are plain gray in winter, but they blush a misty red in early spring. That's when dainty blossoms decorate the leafless stems. Red, dangling winged fruit follows the flowers shortly before rosy leaf buds appear. Green leaves unfurl next, and by summer the tree's canopy is thick with large, shady foliage. If you've got even one red maple in your landscape, autumn will give you bragging rights when leaves turn shades of scarlet or bright orange before dropping.

Young trees need regular water through their first hot season, but red maples that have been in place for a year or more rarely require much

## Acer rubrum

Also sold as scarlet maple, soft maple, swamp maple
Not to be confused with another tree known as swamp maple (*Acer rubrum* var. *drummondii*), which thrives in rare-frost and frost-free areas but has unreliable autumn color

### GETTING ACQUAINTED

Deciduous tree (bare in winter)

40 to 60 feet high by 30 to 40 feet wide

Big leaves turn bright colors in autumn; red flowers and fruit in spring; full canopies oval to rounded

Rapid rate of growth

Resistant to insects and disease

Drought tolerant

Native

Full sun, partial shade, and all-day shade

Any soil, wet or dry, except extremely alkaline

Good choice for parking areas, street trees, shade trees, wooded areas, and wet, boggy spots including ditches, drainage areas, flood zones, lakesides and pond banks; not for azalea beds

Pairs well with liriope, periwinkle, beautyberry, and bridalwreath spirea in dry soil and with Siberian iris and elephant ear in wet soil

Zones 3–9

The more sun a red maple receives, the brighter its autumn color will be. These trees are 'October Glory' red maples.

## NAMED SELECTIONS

'AUTUMN BLAZE': the name says it all

'BOWHALL': orange to red-orange autumn foliage, compact canopy

'COLUMNARE': narrow canopy, vertical form, may grow 70 feet tall

'OCTOBER GLORY': bright orange autumn leaves, even in hot regions where there's little autumn color

## AVOID SILVER MAPLES

Don't confuse red maples (*Acer rubrum*) with silver maples (*Acer saccharinum*). Both are common in the marketplace. Silver maples grow even faster than red ones, but their wood is weak, making trees messy and short-lived. Silver maple branches and even whole trees may split and fall in high winds or ice storms, so you're better off with red maples or sugar maples (*Acer saccharum*).

## DELICATE BARK

Never use string trimmers near tree trunks. Maples have particularly delicate bark. Wounds in trunks can expand and adversely affect a maple's health. When bark wounds encircle the trunk, the tree is said to be "girdled" and it will eventually die.

**A**

**B**

**C**

attention. Red maples do not require pruning, though you can remove lower branches if you need the space. You're better off with a named selection rather than *Acer rubrum* if you're planting trees near places where cars or people need access. Most named selections feature compact crowns of foliage.

Red maples do have a few potential drawbacks. These trees have shallow roots, making it difficult to grow grass or azaleas beneath them. Also, red maples should not be planted beneath overhead lines. If you do, utility companies will eventually ruin the trees' shape with severe pruning in order to keep lines clear of branches. And yes, you'll have to rake in autumn. But maple leaves are great for composting—earthworms love them.

**(A)** Heat, glare, too much water or too little—red maples will take whatever you dish out.
**(B)** Red maples are known for producing lush foliage even when roots are growing in dry, sun-baked soil. Even the stems of leaves are red.
**(C)** The winged seeds of red maple have a red tint.

# Sugar Maple

Though we can't compete with the autumn colors of New England, we can grow one of its signature autumn trees throughout much of the South. The sugar maple is known for turning brilliant shades of gold and orange before leaves drop for the winter. Though an extended Southern summer may commandeer the autumn months, most sugar maples will gamely remain green until a good cold snap gives them an incentive to turn traditional autumn shades.

Sugar maples are large trees, and they cast a broad canopy of high shade. This means that sugar maple branches are usually high enough to walk beneath: Think of a park with picnic tables set beneath large, leafy trees, and you get the idea. Sugar maples usually have a single, solid trunk topped with an oval or rounded crown. Though they grow slowly, these trees top 70 feet. It is imperative that you plant them away from overhead lines. Because the sugar maple's canopy is high, enough sunlight can usually reach the ground beneath the canopy to grow grass successfully, as long as mower blades are set high to avoid nicking protruding tree roots. Sugar maples are great for the estate look of a rolling lawn populated with large, stately trees here and there.

These are the trees found in calendar photos of country lanes; they're also the same trees that are tapped by folks up north who make maple sugar. Urban conditions—pollution, reflected heat from paving, confined root spaces—are detrimental to sugar maples, so they're not a good choice for downtown trees. They are well suited for rural areas, large lots, and parks. Where several small suburban backyards meet, a single sugar maple can be shared, providing shade for all—if the neighbors don't

*Acer saccharum*

Also sold as rock maple, hard maple

**GETTING ACQUAINTED**

Deciduous tree (bare in winter)

60 to 80 feet high by 40 to 50 feet wide

Provides leafy shade in summer; autumn color is outstanding

Slow rate of growth

Not good for urban areas

Full sun is best, tolerates partial shade

Thrives in slightly acidic moist soil with good drainage; tolerates poor soil as long as it is not wet or compacted; not for alkaline areas (limestone)

Ideal as lawn trees, good for lining long rural driveways

Pairs well with lawns that aren't mowed too short; attractive with burning bush and nandina

Zone 4 to upper zone 8

The leafy canopies of sugar maples make them shade tree favorites.

*Trees: Shade*

'BONFIRE': fiery orange-red leaves in autumn
'GREEN MOUNTAIN': known for its scarlet
autumn color and resistance to sun scorch
'LEGACY': known for its heat tolerance

## SUGAR NOT SILVER

Sugar maples grow slowly and have strong wood, earning them the additional common names of hard maple or rock maple. Don't confuse sugar maples with silver maples. The latter is a fast-growing tree often sold cheaply. Not only will you sacrifice autumn color if you buy a silver maple instead of a sugar, but you'll also end up with an inferior tree. The silver maple's rapid rate of growth results in weak wood that's prone to split in storms. Due to a short lifespan, an overgrown silver maple is hazardous and likely to fall.

The botanical names of these two trees add to the confusion: Sugar maple is *Acer saccharum* and silver maple is *Acer saccharinum*. The way to keep them straight is to remember that the one with the "i" in its name is the silver maple, which also has an "i" in it. That's the one you *don't* want. Though the leaves are similar, the silver maple leaf has more finely cut lobes and pale undersides. The sugar maple leaf is the one featured on the Canadian flag and penny.

## WHERE COLD SNAPS ARE RARE

In frost-free areas, substitute red maple (*Acer rubrum*) or Florida maple (*Acer barbatum*). The Florida maple thrives in the heat of lower zone 8 and zone 9. Its oval crown is similar to that of the sugar maple, but its autumn color is not as dramatic. This tree is also sold as *Acer saccharum* var. *floridum*.

mind sharing the task of raking leaves, that is. Sugar maples drop quantities of large leaves in autumn. Maple leaves are excellent for composting. Trees are bare in winter. Spring brings seeds twirling down like little helicopters from above.

A

B

TREES: SHADE

C

D

F

G

E

H

(A) Sugar maples shine in autumn when leaves turn.
(B) Sugar maples are long-lived trees that get large, up to 80 feet high.
(C) When planted as stand-alone trees in the sun, sugar maples develop evenly shaped crowns.
(D) Sugar maples are good choices for planting along the southeastern sides of houses. Dense foliage provides cooling shade in summer and bare branches permit winter sunlight to warm rooms within.

(E) All maples have shallow roots, making it difficult to grow shrubs beneath them. Avoid planting azaleas anywhere within the spread of a maple, as these shallow-rooted shrubs will get cheated out of water and nutrients by the stronger network of tree roots near the soil surface. Dogwoods suffer a similar fate when planted beneath maples.
(F, G, AND H) The autumn foliage colors of sugar maple range from yellow and orange to shades of red.

# Groundcovers

## *Liriope muscari*

Also sold as monkey grass, blue lily turf Not to be confused with mondo grass (*Ophiopogon japonicus)*, which has dark green narrow foliage and thrives in shade

### GETTING ACQUAINTED

Evergreen groundcover

12 to 18 inches high and wide

Clumps of arching foliage last year-round; purple flowers in summer

Rapid rate of growth

Tolerates drought

All-day sun to mostly shady and anything in between

Any soil that's not wet; dry soil is fine

Good choice for narrow spaces, edging beds, filling empty areas, planting near patios, walkways, driveways, paths, low decks, parking areas, in front of taller plants, and as mass plantings

Pairs well with everything except bog plants

Zones 6–10

A single row lining a picket fence makes liriope a good cottage garden plant, too. Note how the liriope makes a tidy transition from garden to sidewalk.

# *Liriope*

If only there were a wardrobe equivalent of liriope. This plant goes with everything. You can dress it up or go casual. Liriope is inexpensive, never out of season, and foolproof. When your garden hasn't got a thing to wear, liriope is the answer.

The leaves of this plant are pliable, narrow, and arching like the foliage of some tropical lilies. When grown beside something lacy and delicate, liriope takes on a rather spiky look—a nice contrast. But when the same liriope is grown in a big bed filled with more of the same, the overall appearance is quite fluffy. The plants blend together like a swath of green fur. Homeowners who are used to thinking of liriope as a plant only suitable for lining up single file to march in circles around trees are sometimes astonished to realize that the big beds of fluff they admire are the same plant, just a lot more of it.

Though frostbite can yellow plants somewhat, liriope foliage rarely loses much of its green color during the mild winters of the South. A generous helping of liriope can do a lot to keep the landscape from fading away during cold months when perennials are asleep, annuals are dead, and many trees and shrubs are leafless. Though liriope is grown for its foliage, not its flowers, this doesn't mean the blooms aren't pretty. Most kinds of liriope produce small spikes decorated with lavender to purple flowers in summer. A few selections bloom white. Flowering may occur in autumn on variegated liriope. By winter, the flowers have been replaced with glossy black berries. The once upright spikes droop under the weight of the fruit.

A

B

C

Grow liriope in sun, shade, and anywhere in between. Plants grow quickly in loose, fertile soil. They'll thrive in poor or compacted soil, too, though spreading may not be as speedy. Liriope usually stays lush with rainfall alone, though it's fine to water sparingly if you want. As clumps grow denser with age, multiple plants will blend together, choking out weeds. This groundcover doesn't mind crowded roots, so you can grow it in confined spaces, such as cutouts in patios or in pots. Liriope is undeterred by reflected heat from paving, hot afternoon sun, and even nearby tree roots. Shade is no problem, either, so there are few restrictions on where to grow liriope. Either moist or dry soil will do, though wet soil is unsuitable.

Liriope is a clumping groundcover, which means it doesn't send out runners the way many shade-loving groundcovers do. Instead, liriope spreads by growing baby plants that come up from the roots, making clumps thicker and wider. Dividing clumps isn't necessary to keep liriope vigorous, but it is a good way to get more plants.

Conventional wisdom holds that it's silly to pay good money for liriope when you can simply dig some up from somebody else's garden. Thinned clumps replenish quickly, making liriope easy to share. Slice through dense plants with a sharp shovel blade any time of year. It is best to move plants between similar settings; liriope that's been growing in shade may be stunned to find itself suddenly growing in the sun, especially if moved during the heat of summer. But even minimal watering can help overcome transplant shock in these tough plants. Once settled, liriope is self-reliant and nearly indestructible.

I find the old faithful solid-green liriope indispensable for the beautiful way it complements other plants—there's no such thing as too much green liriope. It's like the matte inside a picture frame that shows off a

(A) A generous curve of liriope surrounding taller plants makes this common groundcover perfectly at home in a sophisticated landscape.
(B) Lavender flowers are another benefit of liriope, which is also known as monkey grass.
(C) The glossy black berries of liriope persist through winter.

**(D)** Variegated liriope is showy, so it should be planted as an accent in lesser quantities than the solid-green form.

**(E)** Green liriope is an easy choice for giving beds a layered look. It makes a contrasting foreground for dwarf crimson barberry and purple coneflower in this sunny garden.

**(F)** Replace a single row of liriope with a widened sweep of greenery that emphasizes the shape of the planting bed, whether curved or angled.

**(G)** Line walkways with liriope carefully to avoid crowding the paving with overgrown plants later on. Short, straight walks like this one are attractive when bordered, but long, winding paths can end up looking overdone.

## TOMAYTO, TOMAHTO

There's some confusion about liriope's name. Plenty of people call it monkey grass, a name I particularly like and would love to know the story behind. But others apply this same nick-name to *Ophiopogon japonicus*, a different grasslike groundcover that has much skinnier blades that are darker green. In our climate, *Ophiopogon* is better suited for shade than sun, so be careful with the monkey business.

Many gardeners simply say "la-rie-oh-pee," while others pronounce it "leery-ope," to rhyme with "rope." Then there's my mother, who combines the two: "leery-oh-pee." My own pronunciation varies for no good reason. Seeing as how Latin is a dead language, I'm not sure it matters as long as you get home with the right plant. Plant tags sometimes include the name lily turf, but I've never, ever heard a homeowner call it that.

## TO MOW OR NOT TO MOW

Cutting back liriope is a yearly rite of passage for some homeowners. Others never bother. While it is true that trimming this groundcover does promote lush, fresh growth, uncut plants are not likely to decline for want of a haircut. The main things to remember about mow-ing liriope is that the mower blade must be set very high and the job must be completed before new leaves emerge naturally in spring. If you wait too late, skip cutting altogether. The point is to remove last year's old foliage to make plenty of room for new leaves. But a too-late trim damages this year's young leaves. Liriope that has been mowed too late in the season will bear scars all year: browned leaf tips that are blunt instead of rounded or pointy.

D

E

F

G

painting to its best advantage. The green kind is usually sold as *Liriope muscari* though named selections with green foliage include 'Majestic' and 'Big Blue', among others. Don't buy just a few plants of green liriope, get a lot. On the other hand, the variegated selections of liriope, though wildly popular, should be purchased with restraint. The yellow striped leaves of *L. muscari* 'Variegata' are accents themselves, not companions for showcas-ing other plants, so plan accordingly and plant sparingly. Some varieties have foliage that's striped with white or cream instead of yellow and that's a little easier to work into the landscape. *Liriope muscari* 'Silvery Sunproof' and *Liriope spicata* 'Silvery Dragon' are two white-striped cultivars that are available at many nurseries. But even these variegated selections are not subtle and are best positioned near plenty of dark green so the striped leaves can draw the attention they crave. Don't place variegated liriope where it will have to compete visually with other showy plants.

GROUNDCOVERS

# Sundrops Primrose

*Oenothera perennis*

Also sold as yellow evening primrose, common sundrops, narrow-leaf evening primrose, *Oenothera pumila, Oenothera fruticosa glauca, Oenothera fruticosa youngii* Not to be confused with Missouri primrose (*Oenothera missourensis*), which has yellow flowers that open at night

**GETTING ACQUAINTED**

Perennial deciduous groundcover

12 to 20 inches high by 8 inches wide

Bright yellow flowers open on stalks in summer; forms spreading colonies

Rapid rate of growth

Tolerates heat, sun, drought, and poor soil

Resistant to insects and disease

May be invasive

All-day sun to mostly sunny

Dry to average soil; not for wet soil

Good choice for parking areas, sunny patios, hot sunny beds beyond reach of a hose, mailbox plantings, ditches, natural areas, meadows, on slopes, in rock gardens, along roadsides; suitable for beach houses

Pairs well with black-eyed Susan, purple coneflower, liriope, garlic chives, lantana, Queen Anne's lace, nandina, crepe myrtle, rosemary, Anthony Waterer spirea, glossy abelia, autumn joy sedum, autumn sun coneflower, and succulents

Zones 5–9

When the previous owners of my house decided to replace a messy pea gravel driveway with concrete, the contractor shoved quite a bit of gravel into the bed beside the new drive and covered it with a thin layer of excess soil. The resulting mixture of rocks and poor soil baked in the sun, and the spot became prime real estate for weeds.

Fortunately, a neighbor invited me along to dig up a few sundrops primroses. Though the area beside my driveway is not within reach of a hose, I gamely chipped away at the stony soil and planted the sundrops primroses there, figuring if the plants didn't make it, I wasn't out anything but time. I did concede to toting a watering can to my new plants once or twice, but using skepticism to justify my laziness, I kept my efforts to a bare minimum.

I'm a believer now. Sundrops primrose is one tough sun-lover. It cheerfully tackled the rocky, hot, dry, compacted soil and won. Just a few plants eventually spread to cover the ground with small rosettes of triumphant foliage. Each summer, stalks emerge to hold aloft multitudes of buttercup-yellow flowers. The blooming bed looks like a swarm of golden butterflies. All I have to do is cut the empty stalks in late summer or autumn if I feel like tidying up the place. (It's important to cut dried stalks, not pull them, or you're likely to pull up the plants' roots.)

During the first few growing seasons as my sundrops were spreading, I occasionally pulled wild violets up by the roots to give my yellow flowering perennials a fighting chance. That's all they needed to claim the bed as their own. Even a clump of mint growing at one end of the bed is nicely contained by the sundrops primroses' vigorous root system. In fact, I'd

Cheerful yellow sundrops primrose thrives in heat, sun, drought, and poor soil.

*Groundcovers*

## NOT SOLD IN THE GARDEN DEPARTMENT

My umbrella is one of my favorite gardening tools. You can go to a lot of effort to dig up plants, move them, dig new holes, plant your latest acquisitions, and water them only to watch your transplants wilt and die. The most common culprit in such a sad scenario is the sun. Fresh transplants are susceptible to stress. A little hot sunshine can easily push them beyond the permanent wilting point, from which there is no return.

That's when an umbrella or two comes in handy. Keep transplants moist and shaded while they're awaiting planting. Then, as soon as you've got them planted in their new location, give them a drink of water and position an opened umbrella to provide instant shade. Protecting newly moved plants from hot sun is critical during the first few hours after planting, even if the species is a sun-loving plant.

## EVENING PRIMROSE

Also sold as pink primrose, Mexican pink primrose, and *Oenothera speciosa* var. *berlandieri*, the evening primrose is a close relative of sundrops primrose. It also grows in full sun and dry soil and needs little water. The flowers are shell pink and prolific in summer. Evening primrose can be grown from seeds or transplants. Keep seeds and seedlings evenly moist until foliage thickens. After that, rainfall will suffice. Like its yellow-flowering cousin, pink evening primrose disappears in winter and returns in spring, although plants may decline and die after several years. Evening primrose spreads rapidly, especially if grown in moist, fertile soil.

A

B

(A) The blossoms borne in clusters on stem tips are slightly cupped.
(B) Sundrops primrose is an eager spreader. Running roots yield new plants. Make sure you've got plenty of room for sundrops to multiply or solid barriers to contain their growth.

probably be doing battle with the primroses to keep them from taking over the entire garden except for the fact that the driveway stops their spread on one side, steel edging slows them down on the other, and the lawn-mower gets whatever plants creep under the edging into the grass.

To add sundrops primrose to your own garden, choose a spot that's hot and sunny. The more sun, the better. Plants require good drainage, so save naturally moist soils for some pickier species. Slopes, rock gardens, and hot areas beside paving are excellent sites for this durable spreading plant. Foliage fades away to little or nothing in winter. You can cover beds with a thin coat of pine straw if you like, but mulch isn't necessary to protect the cold-hardy roots. Share plants with friends by digging up clumps of foliage and roots. Young transplants moved during hot weather need supplemental watering to help them adjust to their new location. If you're buying sundrops, look for flats or small containers, as there's no need to invest in large plants. Sundrops primrose will quickly spread by its creeping underground roots.

Vines

*Gelsemium sempervirens*

Also sold as Carolina jessamine, yellow jessamine; sometimes mistakenly labeled Carolina or yellow jasmine

**GETTING ACQUAINTED**

Evergreen vine

20 to 25 feet high, sprawling

Buttery, trumpet-shaped blossoms; shiny green foliage

Rapid rate of growth

Tolerates heat and drought

Resistant to insects and disease

Native

All-day sun, mostly sunny, or partially shaded; no need to protect from afternoon sun

Any soil

Good choice for arbors, trellises, fences, posts, rails, and dressing up blank walls; fine for blocking views, adding privacy, and concealing utilitarian structures; will not damage wooden structures

Not for formal gardens due to shaggy shape; flowers may attract wasps, so keep away from swimming pools and children's play areas

Pairs well with crepe myrtle, sundrops primrose, glossy abelia, autumn joy sedum, Queen Anne's lace, and Mexican bush sage

Zones 7–9

Fast-growing Carolina yellow jessamine provides leafy shade and springtime flowers without damaging wooden structures.

# Carolina Yellow Jessamine

The best thing about this vine is its enthusiasm. With very little encouragement, Carolina yellow jessamine swarms up whatever structure is handy and piles on layers of growth to form a leafy canopy at the top. This vine grows rapidly, making it a very satisfying plant to add to your garden. But it is also difficult to keep tidy. During hot weather, long tendrils sprout from the leafy tangle seemingly overnight. This habit gives the vine a decidedly hairy appearance. The best way to handle such behavior is to plant Carolina yellow jessamine where a sprawling, green, wild-haired vine fits into the landscape. Such a strategy saves hours of futile pruning. If you plant this vine thinking an occasional haircut will keep it neatly groomed, you'll soon find that you're mistaken. Carolina yellow jessamine's natural exuberance is better celebrated than contained.

Carolina yellow jessamine has a lot to offer in addition to fast and easy growth. Its foliage stays green year-round, so there'll never be any bare creeping stems to contend with. Privacy enhanced by this vine's presence will not be compromised in winter, and poor views will remain concealed. During particularly harsh winters in zone 7 some foliage may drop, but the loss isn't conspicuous. Warm weather will bring a flush of fresh growth to thicken the canopy again.

In mid to late spring, Carolina yellow jessamine is covered with buttery, trumpet-shaped blossoms. The yellow flowers nestled among the bright green leaves are quite showy. The more sun your vine gets, the heavier it will flower. Full sun also means maximum capacity growth, so plan ahead and give this plant room to sprawl.

A

B

Carolina yellow jessamine has two additional features that are quite endearing. First, it is tough, amazingly tough. It will grow in any kind of soil, from wet to dry, alkaline to acid. It is extremely drought tolerant and is not damaged by insects or disease. This vine isn't bothered by reflected heat from paving and doesn't mind confined roots, which means you can grow it in a little cutout in paving. It is an excellent choice for planting in minimal soil at the foot of posts supporting an arbor above a patio. You can also have a planting pocket left between garage bays or doors when pouring a driveway. A single Carolina yellow jessamine planted there can be trained along a wire strung across the top of both bays. This trick adds refreshing greenery and charm to an otherwise hot, uninviting space. If it is too late to change the configuration of your driveway, put a large pot between the bays and plant the vine there. You can also place pots on patios and decks for growing Carolina yellow jessamine, but vines will require a little more water in containers than they do in the ground. Mulch potted vines for winter, stop watering, and wrap the pots with old blankets during extended freezes. This is necessary because roots in containers are less protected than underground roots.

This vine's other worthy characteristic is that it does not damage wood or masonry. Carolina yellow jessamine grabs onto supports with twining tendrils. It doesn't adhere to surfaces with aerial rootlets the way English ivy infamously does. In fact, Carolina yellow jessamine needs something to grasp. When grown against a flat surface, you'll need to provide a string or trellis for this vine to twine around to get it started growing upward.

You can plant a Carolina yellow jessamine at the foot of a retaining wall and tie a string to stakes at the top and bottom of the wall. The vine will crawl up the string and establish itself as a thick, leafy mass at the top, creating the illusion of a vine that's growing above the wall and cascading gracefully down from the top. The lower stems are without leaves,

(A) The blossoms of Carolina yellow jessamine resemble golden trumpets. More sun means more flowers.
(B) You won't have to wait long for a thick canopy of foliage to grow overhead, though leaves near the ground will always be sparse. Carolina yellow jessamine remains green throughout the seasons.

Carolina yellow jessamine happily tolerates confined root conditions, as this vine thriving in a flowerpot attests. Summer foliage is a rich, shiny green.

## SUPPORT SYSTEM

I advise clients to use disconnected electrical wire to train twining vines horizontally along structures, across walls, or above doors and entries. The coated wire won't rust and mar the surface to which it is attached. Electrical wire is available in dark brown and black, which tend to recede into the scenery. But if you're growing the vine along a light-colored surface, you can use white electrical wire, instead. This support isn't conspicuous while in place but not yet covered by foliage. When fastened securely, it is unlikely to break under the weight of a mature vine.

so many people never notice that the vine is actually rooted in place at the bottom of the wall. This unusual growth habit also means that, even though Carolina yellow jessamine sprawls vigorously, it is unlikely to ever completely conceal a chain link fence. The bottom portion of the fence will remain exposed while the top will be covered in a big mound of foliage and stems.

# Sweet Autumn Clematis

Here's an easy-to-grow vine that likes sun, heat, and neglect. Sweet autumn clematis grows in almost any kind of soil, including wet, dry, fertile, poor, acidic, or alkaline. Heavy clay soils should be amended with a combination of peat and sand to improve drainage prior to planting. This vine climbs by twining, so it won't damage wood or masonry. Though it loses all or most of its leaves in winter, sweet autumn clematis flushes green again every spring. You can let the new growth mound over browned stems, or you can cut the plant back hard after last frost. Unlike some clematis species that bloom on old wood, *Clematis flammula* produces flower buds on new growth, so pruning to encourage fresh sprays makes this vine bloom with increased vigor. Trimming vines before leaves appear will result in lush foliage and the fullest flower show.

The blossoms of sweet autumn clematis are small, but there are thousands of them and they all open pretty much at once. The effect is spectacular. The multitudes of starry flowers coat the vine like great drifts of foam. Flowering occurs from early to mid-autumn, adding some pep to worn-out summer gardens. The show lasts for about three weeks. If you're careful to purchase the species *Clematis flammula*, you'll enjoy heavenly fragrance from the blossoms, too.

Virgin's bower, another clematis sold under three different species names (*Clematis paniculata, C. maximowicziana,* or *C. ternifolia*), looks so much like *C. flammula* that it is often labeled as sweet autumn clematis, too. Both vines are very easy to grow and both bloom prettily in the autumn. But if you want fragrance, look at the Latin. It is easy to remember that the clematis species that starts with "f" (*flammula*) is the fragrant

## *Clematis flammula*

Also sold as fragrant virgin's bower, fragrant clematis
Not to be confused with virgin's bower, which is sold as Japanese clematis (*Clematis paniculata, C. maximowicziana,* or *C. ternifolia*) and may also be labeled as sweet autumn clematis

### GETTING ACQUAINTED

Deciduous vine (bare in winter)

10 to 15 feet high, sprawling

Layers of green leaves are topped with thousands of fragrant, starry blossoms in early autumn

Rapid rate of growth

Tolerates heat and drought

Resistant to insects and disease

May become invasive, especially if virgin's bower is planted by mistake

All-day sun, mostly sunny, or partial shade; no need to protect from afternoon sun

Any soil; must improve drainage when planting in heavy clay

Good choice for arbors, wooden fences, metal fences, trellises, porches, outbuildings, and lampposts; will not damage wooden structures

Pairs well with autumn sun coneflower, autumn joy sedum, garlic chives, rosemary, Mexican bush sage, bronze fennel, nandina, and glossy abelia

Zones 4–10

Sweet autumn clematis is an excellent choice for decorating trellises. For beach houses, look for *Clematis flammula* var. *maritima*.

A

B

C

D

E

one. Virgin's bower is the clematis that yields masses of nearly identical but unscented flowers. It blooms about two weeks before the scented clematis and is the more aggressive of the two vines. Virgin's bower climbs into trees, over other plants, and will spread along the ground. Many gardeners grow it anyway, positioning the plant carefully where it can spread at will, such as along an alleyway or topping a long fence. But it's important to realize that Virgin's bower self-seeds with abandon. Some homeowners cut off the sprays after flowers fade to prevent them from setting seed. Others mow over seedlings or dig them up and give them away. Sweet autumn clematis is listed as an invasive species in some states, and confusion exists as to which vine is the banned one.

Fragrant sweet autumn clematis, sometimes called fragrant virgin's bower, is an energetic grower, too. But it is less likely to grow crazy in full sun the way the unscented plant does. The sweet-smelling vine grows about 10 to 15 feet high and wide if given the opportunity; the unscented virgin's bower can ramble twice as far. Both vines produce seedlings, but the fragrant species may be a little less prolific. For both, flowering is maximized in full sun, so seed production is, too. Conversely, the more shade either vine receives, the fewer flowers you'll get but the fewer seedlings you'll have to contend with. Half-day's sun or dappled sunlight is a good setting for plentiful blooms—enough to admire but not a traffic-stopping show—and only occasional seed germination. You don't have to protect either fragrant sweet autumn clematis or unscented virgin's bower from afternoon sun, so it doesn't matter which half of the day is sunny and which half is shady. Both plants are quite drought tolerant, although virgin's bower is the tougher of the two. If you dig up a plant from the side of the road chances are, its virgin's bower, a Japanese plant that has escaped into the wild and adapted. Fragrant *Clematis flammula* is more likely to be found in nurseries and catalogs.

**(A)** Sweet autumn clematis is a lightweight vine that grows quickly, doesn't damage wood, and blooms in September.
**(B)** An abundance of delicate white flowers cover vines when many other plants are pooped. The species *Clematis flammula* is sweetly fragrant.
**(C)** You can grow sweet autumn clematis as a groundcover, though it may want to climb over nearby plants.
**(D)** The absence of thorns and a tolerance of heat and drought makes sweet autumn clematis a good mailbox plant.
**(E)** Foliage is lush in green in summer but disappears in winter.

## Lonicera sempervirens

Also sold as red honeysuckle, coral honeysuckle
Not to be confused with Japanese honeysuckle (*Lonicera japonica*), which spreads rampantly, or trumpet creeper (*Campsis radicans*), an aggressive, heavy vine that produces large, orange-red flowers

### GETTING ACQUAINTED

Deciduous vine (nearly evergreen in mild winters)

Up to 15 feet high, sprawling

Red, trumpet-shaped flowers appear in quantity in spring and sporadically throughout hot seasons until frost; rounded blue-green leaves

Moderate early growth followed by rapid later growth

Tolerates heat and drought

Native and noninvasive

All-day sun, mostly sunny, or partial shade; no need to protect from afternoon sun

Any soil that's well drained

Good choice for mailboxes, arbors, wooden fences, metal fences, trellises, porches, outbuildings, lampposts, and pole-mounted birdfeeders; include in wildflower gardens, butterfly and hummingbird gardens, natural areas or grow beside patios, decks, and swimming pool decks; grow it in containers but provide support for climbing; will not damage wooden structures

Pairs well with crepe myrtle, Kwanzan cherry, Anthony Waterer spirea, bridalwreath spirea, butterfly bush, glossy abelia, Flower Carpet® rose, burning bush, nandina, Heller holly, rosemary, black-eyed Susan, purple coneflower, candytuft, creeping phlox, bee balm, daisy, Queen Anne's lace, Siberian iris, and Mexican bush sage.

Zones 5–9

Trumpet honeysuckle forms a loosely climbing mound of vining stems. You may need to occasionally twine the stems or tie them to supports to keep vines growing upward.

# Trumpet Honeysuckle

Though the name honeysuckle can strike fear into the heart of Southerners who've battled the invasive Japanese species, the trumpet honeysuckle is a much milder mannered vine. It is well worth getting to know. Trumpet honeysuckle isn't aggressive and it doesn't self-seed. This vine stays right where you plant it, leaning on posts or fences as it grows. Though it is a sprawling vine, you won't find trumpet honeysuckle choking other plants, taking over trees, or gobbling up ground space.

Two-inch red flowers shaped like trumpets (you saw that one coming) decorate the vine in mid-spring. After an initial show of blossoms, trumpet honeysuckle will continue flowering here and there until frost. That's good news for hummingbird lovers—the tiny birds crave the nectar of these red flowers. In fact, if you take a look at plastic hummingbird feeders, most of them are made to resemble oversized trumpet honeysuckle blossoms. Butterflies are attracted to this flowering vine, too. But we gardeners can't have everything: Trumpet honeysuckle is far superior to Japanese honeysuckle in all aspects except fragrance. The red-flowering vine has none, while the yellow- and white-flowered Japanese invader bears heavy perfume.

Grow trumpet honeysuckle wherever you need to dress up something vertical. Fences, lampposts, pole-mounted birdfeeders, trellises, and mailboxes are good spots for this vine. So are overhead arbors and arches. Trumpet honeysuckle is a leaning climber, so you'll have to drape the first few sprays around a support to get it going. Provide a trellis, ladder, or wire to train this pretty vine against a blank wall. With no clingy aerial rootlets, trumpet honeysuckle won't damage wood, brick, or mortar. Though Chinese wisteria and trumpet creeper have given vines a bad name by becoming so woody and heavy that they crush whatever supports them, trumpet honeysuckle remains lightweight.

A

B

C

(A) The tubular red blossoms with yellow interiors are natural hummingbird attractors. No wonder so many plastic feeders feature a similar design.
(B) The long buds of trumpet honeysuckle are colorful and showy before flowers open.
(C) Mild-mannered trumpet honeysuckle is not to be confused with the sweetly scented but terribly invasive Japanese honeysuckle, which should never be planted.

### BUTTERFLY BABIES

If you notice pale green, ridged caterpillars with rosy topsides dining on your trumpet honeysuckle, leave them alone. They are the larvae of spring azures (*Celastrina ladon*), a blue butterfly that lays eggs on this vine during the warm seasons so caterpillars have a food source after they hatch. If you opt to prune your vine, inspect it first for dull-colored chrysalises attached inconspicuously to the plant. Such cocoons are the year's final batch of spring azure caterpillars. They'll emerge in early spring as full-fledged blue butterflies. Wait until the cocoons are empty before trimming your vine.

### NAMED SELECTIONS

'ALABAMA CRIMSON': rich red
'BLANCH SANDMAN', 'LEO', AND
   'MAGNIFICA': red flowers with
   yellow interiors
'CEDAR LANE': deep red flowers
'Flava': orange flowers
'JOHN CLAYTON' AND 'SULFUREA':
   yellow flowers

Average garden soil is fine for growing this flowering vine. Trumpet honeysuckle will grow in any soil that's not wet—even poor, dry soil will do. Plants grown in clay soil will benefit from a mixture of sand and peat added to the planting hole. You can substitute chunky compost or pine bark for peat. The goal is to keep water from puddling around trumpet honeysuckle's roots. Once planted, new vines need water long enough to coax fresh growth. After that, you can forget about this vine unless your area is struck by a severe drought or the vine is grown in a container. The soil in pots and planters dries out more quickly than the ground, so you'll probably have to supplement natural rainfall a little for pot-grown vines.

Trumpet honeysuckle doesn't require pruning, though you can trim bushy growth back in late autumn to promote new growth in spring. If a cold winter damages vines, wait until after the last frost to cut the plant to within inches of the ground. Chances are good that the roots are fine and the plant will grow again as well as ever.

TRUMPET HONEYSUCKLE

*Vines*

Page numbers in **boldface** are main entries.

**A**

*Abelia* x *grandiflora*, ii, **65–66**
*Acer rubrum*, **115–16**, 118
*Acer saccharum*, 116, **117–19**
*Allium tuberosum*, **23–25**
Anthony Waterer spirea, 10, 23, 26, 29, 39, 41, 44, **49–51**, 57, 73, 76, 93, 105, 125, 136; 'Goldflame', 50; 'Limemound®', 50
Autumn joy sedum, **3–5**, 6, 8, 10, 16, 23, 26, 49, 57, 62, 65, 73, 76, 80, 125, 130, 133
Autumn sun coneflower, **6–7**, 13, 23, 26, 29, 32, 44, 57, 65, 80, 125, 133

**B**

Bee balm, **8–9**, 10, 13, 29, 32, 39, 136
*Betula nigra*, **107–9**
Black-eyed Susan, 8, **10–12**, 13, 21, 23, 29, 31, 32, 39, 41, 42, 43, 44, 49, 62, 65, 76, 87, 125, 136; Native black-eyed Susan, *Rudbeckia triloba*, 11
Bridalwreath spirea, 16, 18, **52–53**, 76, 100, 105, 115, 136
Bronze fennel, 8, 10, 11, **13–15**, 21, 26, 35, 39, 76, 133; children's project, 14
*Buddleia davidii*, **57–58**, 98
Burning bush, **54–56**, 69, 105, 117, 136; 'Compacta', 53; 'Rudy Hagg', 53
Butterfly bush, 6, 8, 10, 13, 14, 23, 26, 32, 35, 49, 51, **57–58**, 59, 62, 73, 80, 81, 98, 105, 136; 'Attraction', 58; 'Black Knight', 58; 'Bonnie', 58; 'Dartmore', 58; 'Fascination', 58; 'Lochinch', 58; 'Orchid Beauty', 58; 'Pink Delight', 58; 'Royal Red', 58; 'White Profusion', 58

**C**

Candytuft, 3, **16–17**, 18, 23, 49, 52, 67, 73, 76, 100, 125, 136

Carolina yellow jessamine, 3, 26, 32, 65, 80, 87, 125, **130–32**
*Clematis flammula*, **133–35**
*Colocasia esculenta*, **39–40**
*Cornus kousa*, **93–94**
Creeping phlox, 3, 16, **18–20**, 21, 23, 49, 52, 73, 76, 100, 136; 'Blue Hills', 19; 'Candy Stripe', 19; 'Coral Eye', 19; 'Emerald Blue', 19; 'Emerald Pink', 19; 'Maiden's Blush', 19; 'Red Wings', 19; 'Scarlet Flame', 19; 'White Delight', 19
Crepe myrtle, v, 21, 29, 41, 44, 52, 62, 65, 69, **87–90**, 97, 98, 113, 125, 130, 136; 'Appalachee', 89; 'Caddo', 89; 'Cherokee', 89; 'Choctaw', 89; 'Fantasy', 89; 'Miami', 89; 'Muskogee', 89; 'Natchez', 89; 'Potomac', 89; 'Seminole', 89; 'Sioux', 89; 'Tonto', 89; 'Tuscarora', 89; 'Tuskegee', 89
x *Cupressocyparis leylandii*, **105–6**

**D**

Daisy, 10, 13, 16, **21–22**, 23, 26, 29, 35, 136; 'Becky', 21; 'Brightside', 22; Ox-eye daisy (*L. vulgare*), 21
*Daucus carota*, **32–34**
Doublefile viburnum, 35, 57, **59–61**, 62
Drake elm, 35, **113–14**, 122

**E**

*Echinacea purpurea*, **29–31**
Elephant ear, 8, 10, 13, 29, 32, 35, **39–40**, 41, 49, 57, 76, 115, 122; 'Black Magic', 38; Giant elephant ear, 38; 'Jack's Giant', 38; 'Malanga', 38; 'Paisley', 38; 'Royal Cho', 38; 'Ruffles', 38; 'Variegated Malanga', 38
*Euonymus alatus*, **54–56**

**F**

Flower Carpet® rose, 5, 29, 32, 34, 35, 41, 49, 59, **62–64**, 93, 95, 105, 136;

'Appleblossom', 62, 64; 'Coral', 64; 'Pink', 63, 64; 'Red', 64; 'Scarlet', 64; 'White', 64; 'Yellow', 64

*Foeniculum vulgare* 'Purpureum', **13–15**

**G**

Garlic chives, 3, 6, 8, 10, 13, 16, 18, 21, **23–25**, 26, 29, 32, 41, 44, 57, 65, 73, 76, 80, 81, 87, 98, 125, 133

*Gelsemium sempervirens*, **130–32**

Ginkgo, 54, **91–92**; 'Autumn Gold', 92; 'Lakeview', 92; 'Maygar', 92; 'Princeton Sentry', 92

*Ginkgo biloba*, **91–92**

Glossy abelia, ii, 3, 23, 41, 49, **65–66**, 69, 80, 87, 98, 107, 125, 130, 133, 136; 'Edward Goucher', 66; 'Prostrata', 66; 'Sherwood', 66

**H**

Heller holly, 3, 16, 18, 23, 49, 57, **73–75**, 76, 136

**I**

*Iberis sempervirens*, **16–17**

*Ilex crenata* 'Helleri', **73–75**

*Iris sibirica*, **35–37**

**J**

*Jasminum nudiflorum*, **69–71**

**K**

Kimberly Queen fern, 10, 23, 29, 39, **41–43**, 44, 49, 62, 65, 76, 80, 87, 122, 125

Korean spice viburnum, 16, 18, 35, **67–68**, 76

Kousa dogwood, 49, 60, 62, **93–94**, 122

Kwanzan cherry, 62, **95–97**, 122, 136

**L**

*Lagerstroemia indica*, v, **87–90**

Lantana, 6, 13, 26, 29, 39, 41, **44–45**, 62, 65, 76, 125; 'Dwarf Pinkie', 45; 'New Gold', 45; 'Samantha', 45; 'Weeping Lavender', 45; 'Weeping White', 45

*Lantana* hybrid, **44–45**

*Leucanthemum* x *superbum* 'Becky', **21–22**

Leyland cypress, 52, 54, 91, **105–6**, 107, 110, 111; Southern red cedar, *Juniperus silicicola* and Eastern red cedar, *J. virginiana*, as hot climate substitutes, 106

Lilac chaste-tree, 23, 26, 57, 65, 87, 94, **98–99**, 122, 125; 'Abbeville Blue', 99; 'Alba', 99; 'Colonial Blue', 99; 'Lilac Queen', 99; 'Mississippi Blue', 99; 'Montrose Purple', 99; 'Rosea', 99

Liriope, 10, 39, 41, 76, 87, 93, 95, 98, 100, 107, 113, 115, **122–24**, 125; 'Big Blue', 124; 'Majestic', 124; *L. spicata* 'Silvery Dragon', 124; 'Silvery Sunproof', 124; 'Variegata', 124

*Liriope muscari*, **122–24**

*Lonicera sempervirens*, **136–38**

**M**

*Magnolia* x *soulangiana*, **100–3**

Mexican bush sage, 3, 6, 7, 8, 18, 21, 23, **26–28**, 32, 65, 69, 80, 81, 98, 105, 130, 133, 136; 'All Purple', 27; 'Midnight', 27; 'Purple Velvet', 27; 'Santa Barbara', 27

*Monarda didyma*, **8–9**

**N**

Nandina, 3, 6, 8, 23, 26, 29, 41, 44, 49, 54, 67, 69, 73, **76–79**, 107, 117, 125, 133, 136; 'Atropurpurea Nana', 78; 'Gulfstream', 78; 'Lowboy', 78; 'Harbor Belle®' 78; Yellow-berried (*N. domestica* var. *leucarpa*), 79

*Nandina domestica*, **76–79**

*Nephrolepis obliterata*, **41–43**

**O**

*Oenothera perennis*, **125–27**

**P**

*Phlox subulata*, **18–20**

*Pinus strobes*, **110–11**

*Prunus serrulata* 'Kwanzan', **95–97**

Purple coneflower, 8, 10, 13, 21, 23, 26, **29–30**, 32, 39, 41, 42, 43, 44, 62, 65, 87, 124, 125, 136; 'White Swan', 31

**Q**

Queen Anne's lace, 8, 9, 13, 23, 29, **32–34**, 39, 44, 62, 80, 125, 130, 136; children's project, 34

**R**

Red maple, 35, 39, 52, **115–16**, 118; 'Autumn Blaze', 116; and avoidance of silver maples, 116; 'Bohall', 116; 'Columnare', 116; 'October Glory', 115, 116

River birch, 65, 76, 105, **107–9**, 110; 'Dura-Heat®', 108; 'Heritage®', 108

*Rosa* Flower Carpet®, **62–64**

Rosemary, 3, 6, 10, 13, 18, 23, 26, 29, 32, 41, 44, 57, 65, **80–83**, 87, 125, 130, 133, 136

  Prostrate: 'Huntington Carpet', 82; 'Irene®', 82; 'Mrs. Howard's Creeping', 82; 'Prostratus', 82; Santa Barbara ('Lockwood de Forest'), 82

  Upright: 'Albus', 82; 'Arp', 82, 83; 'Hill Hardy' ('Madeline Hill'), 82, 83; 'Majorica Pink', 82; 'Tuscan Blue', 82

*Rosmarinus officinalis*, **80–83**

*Rudbeckia fulgida* 'Goldsturm', **10–12**

*Rudbeckia nitida* 'Autumn Sun', **6–7**

**S**

*Salvia leucantha*, **26–28**

Saucer magnolia, 16, 18, 35, 52, **100–3**

*Sedum spectabile* 'Autumn Joy', **3–5**

Siberian iris, 8, 16, 18, 21, **35–37**, 39, 52, 59, 62, 67, 76, 100, 113, 115, 136

*Spiraea* x *bumalda* 'Anthony Waterer', **49–51**

*Spiraea* x *vanhouttei*, **52–53**

Sugar maple, 3, 6, 10, 23, 29, 32, 49, 54, 65, 76, 80, 87, 116, **117–19**; and avoidance of silver maple, 118; 'Bonfire', 118; Florida maple, *Acer barbatum*, as hot climate

substitute, 118; 'Green Mountain', 118; 'Legacy', 118

Sundrops primrose, 16, 41, 44, 98, **125–27**, 130; evening primrose, *Oenothera speciosa* var. *berlandieri*, 126

Sweet autumn clematis, 3, 6, 13, 23, 26, 65, 76, 80, **133–35**; Virgin's bower, 133

**T**

Trumpet honeysuckle, 8, 10, 16, 18, 21, 26, 29, 32, 35, 49, 52, 54, 57, 62, 65, 73, 76, 80, 87, 95, **136–38**; 'Alabama Crimson', 138; 'Blanch Sandman', 138; 'Cedar Lane', 138; 'Flava', 138; 'John Clayton', 138; 'Leo', 138; 'Magnifica', 138; 'Sulfurea', 138

**U**

*Ulmus parvifolia* 'Drake', 35, **113–14**, 122

**V**

*Viburnum carlesii*, **67–68**

*Viburnum plicatum* var. *tomentosum*, **59–61**

*Vitex agnus-castus*, **98–99**

**W**

White pine, 52, 105, 107, **110–11**

Winter jasmine, 26, 54, 65, **69–71**, 76, 87; Florida jasmine, *Jasminum floridum*, 70